THE
WHOL

GW0067468b

'A piercingly beaut
which urges us all to love bravely. This book changed
me. I couldn't put it down.'

'Visceral and meticulous, Norwood's account is an aston-
ishing and unflinching act of remembrance and love.'

'What an incredible book. I don't think I have ever
read anything so delicate – every placement of every
word is perfect.'

'A heartbreakingly brave, candid and lyrical memoir of
baby loss.'

'*The Song of the Whole Wide World* is a tender and poetic
account of unimaginable grief.'

'*The Song of the Whole Wide World* shimmers. Tamarin Norwood's poetic writing is gut-wrenching and gorgeous, all at the same time. It is a story for anyone grappling with the forces of gravity of life and death, of medical decisions, and surrendering to waves of love.'

AMY KUEBELBECK,
author of *A Gift of Time: Continuing Your Pregnancy When Your Baby's Life Is Expected to Be Brief*

'I've never read a book like *The Song of the Whole Wide World*. It's a thrilling act of imagination about mothering that illuminates the body and its metaphysical matters. Tamarin Norwood's writing shows a respect towards her son so pure that I felt both humbled and proud to witness it. I'm still reeling from the piercing pain and joy of this book. Unforgettable.'

GWYNETH LEWIS MBE,
a National Poet of Wales

'A work of great and subtle beauty. It expanded my understanding of life, death and what it means to be a mother.'

CATHY RENTZENBRINK,
author of *The Last Act of Love: The Story of My Brother and His Sister*

'This book took my breath away. It's a journey of love and loss and I'm grateful for Tamarin's gift to write and articulate so tenderly what many bereaved parents cannot.'

NICOLA WELSH,
CEO of Held In Our Hearts,
a charity providing baby loss counselling

THE SONG
OF THE WHOLE
WIDE WORLD

*On Grief, Motherhood
and Poetry*

TAMARIN NORWOOD

THE
INDIGO
PRESS

THE INDIGO PRESS
50 Albemarle Street
London w1s 4bd
www.theindigopress.com

The Indigo Press Publishing Limited Reg. No. 10995574
Registered Office: Wellesley House, Duke of Wellington Avenue
Royal Arsenal, London se18 6ss

First published in Great Britain in 2024 by The Indigo Press

A CIP catalogue record for this book is available from the British Library

First published in 2024

ISBN: 978-1-9116-4873-4
eBook ISBN: 978-1-9116-4874-1

Extract from Berlin, I. 'What'll I Do?' (1923), p.115: From MUSIC
BOX REVUE OF 1924. Words and Music by Irving Berlin, copyright
© 1923 BERLIN IRVING MUSIC CORP. All Rights Administered
by UNIVERSAL MUSIC CORP. All Rights Reserved Used by
Permission. Reprinted by Permission of Hal Leonard Europe Ltd.

Extract from Croft, D. 'Gig and Pony' (1960), p.11: Words and
Music by David Croft. All Rights Reserved Used by Permission.
Reprinted by permission of Worldwide Theatrix Ltd.

Every effort has been made to obtain permission for the
copyrighted material, and the publisher will be glad to make
appropriate acknowledgements at the first opportunity.

Cover design © Tamarin Norwood and Luke Bird
Art direction by House of Thought
Typeset in Goudy Old Style by Tetragon, London
Printed and bound in Great Britain by TJ Books Limited, Padstow

MIX
Paper from
responsible sources
FSC® C013056

GABRIEL
BENEDICT VIESEL

14 December 2018

there flew a sparrow
into the house
and then away

ONE

Look at this, my mother said to me when I was very small. She was opening a pear at the kitchen table. I pressed against her side and watched, and she pulled back the blade and drew apart the halves. In the whole wide world, she said, nobody has ever seen this sight but us.

Small as I was, I understood this moment to be very special, all because it was so simple. Anyone can open up a pear, but the thing is first to know, and then to care, that there is wonder to be found. Here was wonder, and it was ours alone.

She must have quartered the pear and cored it soon enough, and we must have eaten it up, but I don't remember that. I only remember our stillness, the impossible perfection of those finely cut halves, the loving detail of the grainy flesh, the shiny pips and their shiny cases split by the knife and gleaming.

*

I remembered the cut of the pear when we first moved here, and now I think of it often. I think of it when I turn an apple on the tree outside and find it opened by the wasps and mice and sparrows that nibble half the yield. A wonder just missed.

I think of it in the stone wall we pinned the tree against, each stone as old as the house and marked with ivy barbs and stabs of the chisel that shaped it. The stones are so old now, and sit so heavily in time, that it is hard to imagine how bright they must have been when they were first cut from the ground, singing with the split of the chisel and the spit of dust into the air. The quarry is an acre beyond the garden wall, so the singing of the stones would have been heard from here, and the gruff of the horses labouring slabs on wooden carts, and the cries of men too burdened for wonder.

Beyond the quarry where the walnuts grow there used to be an orchard, and its cider press was never taken down. It stands in one of the old stone barns under sagging slate that must let in the rain. I have never seen it, but it is there, and I think of the cut of the pear when I imagine the apples it must have shattered by the hundred, roaring in from buckets and each one crumpling or shearing or splitting its skin uniquely, bursting wet and pips, each one a world unseen.

The quarry fell silent a century ago, and over the years the ridges of stone have softened with clay and soil and now grass tugged up by cattle in the summer months. The cows tread the slopes with ease and do not know the earth is ecstatic beneath them, even if, in their way, they are part of it. But I believe it is. When I walk over the surface of the ground – these hills and trees, the houses put up, the rocks lying under the turf and the animals so quiet – in the fibre of the silence there is a singing to be heard. Or if not singing then restlessness, possibility, bristling almost out of reach.

It is a place so self-contained as to almost be a world of its own, as though its topology were spherical, from our house to the churchyard, the school, the quarry, the fields and the stables and the cows, all making their home as much within the ground as on its surface. Not the smooth-cast round of a planet but the round of a seed, a cob, a nut.

*

Six winters ago, this round of land was cut through by a blade of silver light curving along the roads that crossed it. It was nearly Christmas and the purchase of our house had suddenly gone through. We had hired a van the very same day, thrown what we could into the back and driven into the night, the three of us sitting in a row across the wide front seat: wife and husband and two-year-old between us, head lolling in sleep. At last, the headlights opened before us the kerb of a sloped tarmac path where four darkened cottages fell away from the road. We made our way to the fourth, turned the new key in the lock, found the wall switches one by one, and one by one every room was spun with light.

Then I remember we just stood there, breath visible in the cold, looking. The beaten wood floors, carpet full of dust on the narrow stairs, the tanging echo of empty rooms that made us whisper as though we were there in secret. We travelled up and down the stairs, put our fingers on the windowsills, the taps, the cupboard doors, trod out where the furniture would go. Never since have we seen our home so piercingly, split open before our eyes, being night, being cold and bare, being all ours.

We woke in the morning to thick fog all around, as though the night had turned pale while we were asleep. In shoes that slipped and let in cold we set out to explore. The ground revealed itself in patches as we followed the track through the fog, past where the hills and the orchard must have been, over the stiles and cattle grid and flat stone bridge, the soil frozen hard, long grasses clumped with frost and pressed down by leaves disintegrating and sparkling white. Again we found we were whispering. We followed the track through a weighted gate where two rope fences led the way between sloping paddocks and, with the clap of the gate, horror came. Breath that sounded hot and dark from lungs much too big, then hooves much too close, and I felt for Anatole's little gloved hand and pulled him near. Then two horses, three, rose from the fog, tails flicking – and were away. Anton put Anatole on his shoulders after that and we retreated from the paddocks singing a slow and boisterous rhyme, pitch all out of kilter, until he was settled again:

Gig and pony, gig and pony, trotting along
    the way—

The rhyme took us along a bitten tarmac path to where a homely church stood waiting, the low square tower and all the walls familiar with the stone of our house and the garden wall. We stopped singing and the lovely silence came as a reproach for all our noise, and when we spoke after that every word uttered into the cold air made a daring claim upon the place: we belong here too. We are new and this land is very old, and we are here.

*

But now we know that this is Gabriel's land. His is the churchyard, his the hills and the trees and all they bear, his the gleaming pips and the dark in the lungs of beasts, his the shattering ice and snow, the song, the cold, and all the secrets of the ground.

TWO

Christmas came and went, and we settled into our home and began to see it in the normal way, which was barely to notice it at all, the small rooms inside overcome by toys and books and clutter laid gladly over the wonder of the house like clay and turf over stone.

When Anatole was three I pressed his hand against my navel and asked what he thought might be hiding inside. He guessed correctly, a baby, and this baby he kissed and kissed over and over before returning to his toys. The baby was the reason I had been so sleepy and always lying down, we explained, in case he had noticed and was wondering why. In the days that followed he sauntered through the house with the new information, telling us the plans he was making for the sleeping arrangements of his baby, for the stowing away of dangerous toys, how he would push the pushchair himself, being so strong.

We visited my parents not long after, and stood Anatole on a chair at the head of the table so he could announce to them his proud news. That evening, when he was asleep in the bright little bed my parents had assembled for their grandchildren's visits, we talked about the baby more. The scan had revealed an ambiguous shadow in the region of the baby's abdomen, long and sharp like a spear but soft like a smudge, I thought, as though it might be part of the greyscale image of the baby and not part of the baby itself. We had willingly overlooked the caution in the sonographer's voice when she said it might be nothing. And now, in low voices around the kitchen table there was only a shadow of concern admitted, the little catch to the festivity being another scan the following week.

*

There was indeed another scan, and another and another. Weeks passed and the shadow ceased to be nothing, nor a smudge, nor a spear. It established a form of its own, with outlines firm and clear, and settled among the organs of the baby's abdomen and began to fill them.

Before long, nothing was left of the original

scan but its ambiguity. The mass had density, and measurements captured with cursor on screen, but each scan presented new contradictions. For two weeks or more it was thought to be a teratoma, a tumorous region of growth named after the Greek for *monster* for the full range of human cells it might contain from hair to nail to tooth to part of eye. Such a monster would have ended the baby's life long before it was due to be born, and then the next scan told a story with no monsters but other threats; the next, another story again.

So we passed the summer. We slept very little, saving conversations until Anatole was asleep and then spending the nights at the kitchen table or sleepless in bed looking up new words, probabilities, local provision for social care, advice on bereavement in young children. The thought of the monster had infected me, grey and pale and silent. I had a university library account, we remembered, and we made nightmarish use of it, reading articles in medical journals we hoped would not come true. Everything we learned we learned provisionally. We did not know which ocean we would drown in, but we would drown.

We named the baby Gabriel Benedict, his first name borrowed from my middle name. We tried to do ordinary things. We tended the garden, we went for walks in the late afternoons, a model railway was open and we visited. One Saturday we went to a local museum which we found almost empty: just dark, panelled rooms with ropes across the embroidered seats of hard-backed chairs, leatherwork behind glass, fragile staring dolls, strict wooden games with counters and cards.

In one room a temporary exhibition of a printmaker's work was on display: heavy linocuts of churches and stately homes in black and dull green drawn in both plan and section at once, so the buildings seemed to lie flat in the pools of their grounds. One of the buildings lay in a pool the shape of a pregnant belly emaciated by dwindling amniotic fluid. Where paths and trees reached the outer border of the estate they pushed against it like thin limbs pushing against the skin from inside, and where nothing pushed against the border, here and there it sank in, sallow and dark.

The prints were so unbeautiful. They were sad and cold, no leaves on the trees, no warmth in the hearth, the green in places a screeching whitish yellow. Near the greatest protrusion, which lopsided the belly, flew a dozen leaden birds on the white of the page, but they failed to lift the spirit. The day, the place, the birds were leaden. The artist must have visited on cold damp days, dead leaves and hard mud underfoot, the sky all cloud, lending a factual shadowless and sunless aspect to the place. I was grateful the prints had not pretended otherwise.

I found I was drifting through the rooms of the museum with Gabriel alone – a strange outing just for him and me. A baby and his mother. His mother, conditionally. By now we had been advised by more than one consultant that if Gabriel were neither well enough to live nor sick enough to die, then his life and ours would become as restricted as it was possible to imagine, and interminably so. In our circumstances, they advised, the law would allow us to end the pregnancy at any moment until the birth itself. Just not after the birth. There was silence in the room as we took in this limit. Where the line is drawn.

Late August arrived, and with it a new word to absolve me. *Anhydramnios*. There was no more amniotic fluid, the liquor that protects the baby from heat and cold and shocks from outside movement and gives it space to flex and grow. What there was had been used up, and no more was coming.

We looked up the new word. We read that babies are sometimes said to breathe amniotic fluid in the womb, but real breathing only begins at birth. The events of labour, the new oxygen-rich air, the cutting of the umbilical cord: these things prompt irreversible changes in the respiratory system. Where oxygen once flowed through the placenta and umbilical cord directly into the baby's bloodstream, now an inaugural breath sends a first blush of air from the room of the labour ward all the way to the alveoli, the soft, porous buds at the branching edges of the lungs; the last of the fluid is absorbed, and breathing can finally begin. By the time the first breath is taken, the fluid that had filled the baby's lungs in the womb is almost completely cleared. In the womb, the filling of the lungs with fluid is not breathing, but it is learning to breathe. With no fluid, the baby's lungs fail to grow as they should, and it will only survive its birth by minutes or hours. *Amniotic.* It does not derive from *amnesia*, as I had imagined, but from *lamb*, little lamb.

So this was our ocean.

September came, and in the car to his nursery and in the warm dark of bedtime Anatole ventured his questions and gathered his answers around him.

Over the weeks he tried each question several times in case he could get a more favourable answer or one that was easier to understand. He heard, many times over, that some babies are only *inside babies*, who live their whole lives inside their mothers and cannot live at home even if their family dearly wants them to. He heard that when our baby is born, we will hold him and kiss him. He heard there was something called dying, which he could not understand other than it seemed to mean not being frightened to be closed into a box, buried and left alone. I could not get him to understand that the body and the mind were distinct, and that one would cease to work and would stay to be buried, and one would simply go away, and that this was why Gabriel wouldn't be afraid. I did not want Anatole to be bereaved. I did not want him to have sad parents and a sad house. I did not want him to know his parents planned to put one of their children in a box and leave it outside forever. I worried that this idea would darken his mind in an irreparable way. Perhaps he had not yet made enough world to contain what we were trying to tell him. Three years old is so young, and death so big.

He asked to play a bedtime game almost every night for many weeks. He played the doctor, and used a fabric hippo with soft bells inside to scan my tummy and relate to me that the baby was not well. He waited for my expression of sorrow, which I offered sometimes with real tears and sometimes pretend, then he elaborated: the baby would be born, we would give him kisses, he would die, we would put him in a box and dig him up. Bury him, I corrected. Bury him, he said.

*

It was a lonely ocean, but not unfamiliar to the doctors assigned to our care, who met with us one by one like vessels attending a stricken ship. The purpose of these meetings was to reach a mutually informed agreement for the care of Gabriel until his death. We were grateful for the tenderness with which these conversations rocked and waned to balance the needs of the moment, as analysis gave way to sorrow, to question, to speculation, to sorrow again. We learned that a great deal would remain unknown, how it feels to be born being almost as mysterious to medicine as how it feels to die.

We know that in the womb a baby is sleepy and often asleep, sedated by the low oxygen in its bloodstream and by analgesic hormones that induce sleep and inhibit neural activity. Birth releases the newborn into wakefulness and fullness of feeling at the very moment it is hit by the light and cold and undamped clatter of the world outside. The effort of the first cry is to end this affront and, if met by the embrace of the mother against her skin, miracles of synchrony regulate the temperature, blood pressure, glucose and oxygenation of the newborn, calm its crying and encourage first alertness. To begin with, what comfort the baby can find is drawn from poor simulacra of the uterine environment. It is no longer as warm as in the womb, but it is warm enough; the mother's voice sounds less familiar than when it was heard from within, but familiar enough; likewise her heartbeat, her smell, her rhythms. It is not as dark as it was, but perhaps the light in the room is low, and perhaps eyes can be closed.

If Gabriel's birth was to be a kind of waking up to the day of life, affronted, and then longing for and gradually forgetting the lovely dream of sleep, then would his death be a falling into the sleep of night? Perhaps. Among the doctors we spoke to, the cautious consensus was that his birth would be a greater event for him than his death, which, it was cautiously hoped, would be peaceful. I formed the impression that he might experience the ending of his life as the completion of his recovery from birth: everything would just become less and less difficult for him, less cold, less bright, less noisy, then nothing at all.

But hope was not certainty. Two opinions stood apart from the general consensus. One consultant proposed that we end the pregnancy rather than spend the next months preparing ourselves to watch the little baby choke to death. Another, more measured in his tone, said his death might feel like drowning. It happened that I had been reading about drowning not long before, and knew it to be an awful way to die. Water enters the larynx and the vocal cords constrict, preventing fluid from entering the lungs but restricting the intake of breath completely. Just before asphyxiation the larynx is forced back open in an involuntary attempt to get oxygen at any cost, and the lungs fill with fluid. We did not understand completely how the matter would be reversed if it was not fluid but air that Gabriel would drown in, but we supposed he was describing something awful. We were grateful for the frankness of these consultants. Their brutality of expression was, I believed, no less carefully judged than the tenderness of the other consultants, and no less attuned to the needs of the moment. The possibility of termination was so present in these conversations that letting the pregnancy run its course was decisive in itself. We would not be *letting* him live, we would be *making* him live. We did not know what his shred of life would bring him, and our decision was to make him live.

We did not want any of this for him. We knew what a happy infancy looked like, boisterous and rosy and sensitive, and we wanted it for both our sons, not only one. Nevertheless, between Gabriel's birth and death, we could see a sliver of possibility. It was realistic to hope that he could crest into life and reach some peak of his own, whatever it was, and that this his furthest reach could be so rich and strange and so murkily remarkable to him that even if it was felt in distress it would still be something for him; still more and not less; it would still be life lived. We were going to make him try, poor thing. And so the doctors assembled his little raft of measures. He would not be taken from my arms, the poor simulacrum of my womb. Should he feel pain or the smallest sign of discomfort there would be a suck of sucrose, oxygen by nasal prong, morphine injected subcutaneously. A specialist would attend in case of need. Then his body would keep its secrets, unless we asked of him an autopsy when everything was done.

Back outside the hospital, the sun was bright and warm and there was time to sit on the bench by the door, and there I imagined something completely new. Thick flowers, heavy petals, edges piped with lead or patterned into fabric. I watched the thought, which seemed to have bloomed from nowhere. The fullness of colour, heavy with scent that weighs their tendrilous arms. It was the newest thought I had ever had. How extravagant, how vibrant, to conjure an image with no bearing at all on Gabriel, on us, on the weight of what was to come. There must have been some small abundance of my mind still left over in excess of our immediate needs, from which, briefly and miraculously, there sprang all of a rhododendron, all of a sticky red jasmine, all of the dark bright flowers that make the soil hum in the shadows of yews. Then the thought was gone, as quickly as it had come.

THREE

Now five months into the pregnancy, we could see without ambiguity that Gabriel would not survive his brief cresting into the light of the world.

But by night, the clarity of day was shot through with possibility. In these months the nights were long and wakeful and dark, and full of invention. My body was the whole of his world, I thought, so surely I had within me the means to save him. I would do anything. In the dark my mind turned over and over the same dilemma, searching for a way out. As long as he did not surface he was safe, I thought, like a sort of fish, who would drown in air. I imagined his developing lungs like gills: systems of paper-thin folds held apart by the water that flows between them and so delicate they collapse if brought up into the world. It is as dangerous for a fish to rise to the surface as it is for a person to dive beneath it, and the effort no less great.

Here was a possibility. If the effort and the threat were alike for him and me, then I could reverse it and take on the effort myself. I could learn to dive, to open my eyes and hold my breath underwater, and when he was born he would never need try his lungs, only his gills, and we could dwell together. I knew he could swim; I had seen it in the first of his ultrasound scans, when the grainy dark smudge in his abdomen was yet to be real and all was still well. I heard a radio report around this time of train carriages, at the end of their lives, felled to the sea floor where they become new reefs, their weltered metal walls coralline and pink and suckled by the gaping mouths of fish, doors and windows wide to boneless squid that dart and hide and I thought *there*, we could live there, I could swim down and down and down, never come up, and *there* you would be, and there we would be safe.

On sleepless nights I sent out thoughts like these to probe the furthest depths of hope, of poetry, of science: emergency beacons that one by one returned without news. Whatever outbound route they took there was only one way back, to me, my baby, as close and distant as it was possible to be. He doesn't have gills, he has lungs. All the oxygen in his blood is from my breath. The fluid in my womb is gone. And I have a living son, who needs me on dry land.

These nights revealed me to myself as two distinct terrains: inside, in the dark, rosy and rounded, warm and safe, a pool, an underground lake – and this was where he lived; hemmed all around by the impenetrable bank that is the surface of me – and this was where I lived. I had never so keenly felt that I live on the surface of myself, that my body is shaped to meet what is outside itself and not within. How ill-judged it seemed that my arms, my mouth, my eyes should be out here with me, how poorly planned when there is such fullness, such lively richness, such possibility within.

*

Medicine sends out its own strange probes. One afternoon my mother held my hand as a thick needle was pushed through the taut skin of my belly to extract a little of the scant remaining fluid. Putting my coat on afterwards, I watched the midwife peel two printed labels from a sheet in her file and apply one to each of the plastic vials the needle had supplied. Twin vials, smaller than I had imagined, neat and contained like oxygen tanks. I asked to hold them. Their smooth, even weight was warm against my skin. But for the plastic, but for the span of a minute or so, the cold of the room, the coat done up, I almost held him then.

And there were the inaudible signals of the sonographer's wand, routinely pressed against my abdomen. Once, not long before the birth, I asked a consultant to show me what he could of the baby's face and let me take home a printout. He pressed into my skin and we watched the corresponding greyness take shape obscurely on the screen: That's the bridge of the nose, the forehead, the jaw just here, he said as the indifferent cursor caressed those tender forms. Then he stopped when from somewhere, from me, soft vowels of sorrow filled the room. A tissue was put into my hand and then, I saw, into my husband's too. In the silence that followed the picture was printed, and the attending geneticist explained the features again. It was difficult to make anything out. Her fingertip indicated a prominent curve: That's the forehead, she said. It's a good forehead. I was pleased. I smiled. It *was* a good forehead. What a dear baby. Only later did I recognize what a generous remark this was, and how well placed. She saw that we needed our baby to be admired and adored, and should he die before birth, hers might be the only such remark of all his life. When he resumed the scan I noticed the consultant's eyes were wet too. All of this meant something. But for many things, between us, we almost held him then.

We almost held him in the evenings too, as he grew and his movements became prominent. We would watch the spectacle sadly. When he kicked, the protrusion of his limbs into the very air of the room seemed otherworldly, like dreams pluming from the furthest horizons of our world, and we wished he were real. Yet he was real. It was just that for us, the nature of his realness was impossible to grasp.

I can remember the strange unrealness of Gabriel's older brother before he was born. His had been an easy, healthy pregnancy, and not being able to know the baby or yet believe he was real was a delight, a confection, an adorable quirk of his protean personality. We hadn't named him Anatole yet, he was just *the baby*. There was a song I used to play him in the womb. I would put on this song and sway and dance and sing him the words, and always press my palms against his roundness.

It completed a circle somehow; if I danced without my palms against him it felt as though I was dancing alone.

What a day for a daydream
What a day for a daydreaming boy—

Lazily I used to wonder what Anatole was making of the song, the swaying, the pressure of hands, if he was making anything at all. I didn't know, and it didn't much matter. Whatever imprint these sensations might have made upon the softness of his growing brain were provisional, like promises I made him that would soon come true.

He would certainly have heard something; now I was pregnant again I knew this much. There was nothing lazy about my wondering with Gabriel. I had begun to pore over the dense and difficult papers of medical journals as though they were parenting manuals, trying to grasp as precisely as I could exactly what he was making of his world.

I learned that midway through pregnancy, the growing bones of his inner ear would already be registering vibrations that fell against his eardrum and transmitting their hum through the fluid of the spiral shell cochlea to fine hairs that tap their message against the auditory nerve. What impossibly miniature instruments, and what a strange underwater world they must describe to a growing brain: the close bubbling and pulsing of the mother's inside, her voice heard from within herself, and ambient noise and speaking too, only not as we hear it. Sound from outside is attenuated by the thickness of maternal tissue, which filters out high frequencies that carry the detail of speech. Consonants and many vowels are lost, and what remains is prosody: the rhythms, melodies and personal cadences of language in use. These soft-edged sounds, the most elementary blocks of language, do carry meaning, but for a baby their meaning only comes true after birth, when their familiar sound helps to organize and shape the flow of speech the newborn hears. Although the patterns of prosody are not the same as the patterns of grammar, they are similar enough to guide early discrimination between blocks of meaningful sound, and so language learning begins.

He would have felt the pressing of my palms too. Around the time his hearing developed, his movements would have grown more purposeful in the womb, and shown a preference for touching those parts of his body most densely webbed with nerves: the skin of the face, the nape, the feet. In the last months of pregnancy, when I pressed my palms against my belly he would have moved towards my touch, reaching out a hand to probe the inside of the uterine wall. The mother's touch, like the soft-edged sounds of prosody, carries meaning not yet known to her baby. And just as prosody guides early grammar, this touching should one day come true in proprioception, the baby's awareness of its body in space, and later on of itself in sympathy with others.

Like his brother, I sang and swayed with Gabriel too. It was easy to feel he and I were engaged in a shared project of growing closer and closer together, a kind of neural and cellular falling in love. I imagined the soft-edged sounds of my speech reaching into his world as the soft-edged forms of his limbs reached into mine. I pressed against the uterine wall and imagined him pressing in return, hands meeting palm to palm in dreamlike mirror forms. I sent my songs to him, my movements, my love, and received in return the warmth of the plastic vials, the shadows on the screen, the neural pathways pressing on and on towards me as I pressed and pressed to imagine his underwater world. I took him to places: into woodland, over fields. We spent time in the garden sun. I booked a single seat at a concert for him and me, to show him the resonant depth of the music in the room, then cancelled in case it would be too sad. I imagined the food I ate was a line dropped down to him, the goodness and vestigial flavour of which might be detected in his cells. Once, I sent him a hazelnut:

Dear Gabriel,

Today your kicks have been soft, like warm hazel-nuts in honey. I've been thinking about making a jar of honeyed hazelnuts for your papa. You have to gently toast them first and layer them in a jar with honey and they slightly soften, then you can put a spoonful of them on your porridge in the morning. Perhaps your little mind will form an impression of your papa, if you're alive still when you're born. I am content that you know me. I am the one who's your world.

Here, I will send you a hazelnut:

You see it's crunchy, there's a sort of milky bitter-ness, in my mouth are shreds of the woody coat. You wouldn't know what's in my mouth. But perhaps there is something in you that will take in the goodness—

Thus I sent him words too; not only the sounds of my voice, but writing. I wrote the kinds of words and syntax you would speak with a child, as though he could understand. In this way the writing completed a circle too, as though if I didn't write, I was alone. It was another line dropped down to him, and I knew he would leave this line behind when he was gone. It was a comfort to think I could continue to write to him, just as I was now, after his death. We talk to the dead in their absence; Gabriel's absence was already here.

But in the line it dropped, the writing contributed to a confusion in my mind about the ways in which Gabriel was with us while he was with us. The line seemed to connect me with an imaginary friend I would be able to commune with for as long as I needed him, with only a brief complication at the moment of his birth, before he could be returned safely to my imagination. I knew this to be untrue and I resisted the comfort it brought me. Yet it was impossible to grasp what exactly *was* true of him, and I urgently needed to, before the complication of his birth and the new imaginary turned out not to be the same.

The studies I was reading about foetal development all seemed to observe the period of gestation through a lens positioned at its conclusion: pregnancy seen through the fulfilment of its promise in birth and infancy and the span of new life. Prosody promises grammar, touch promises proprioception, even the mother's attachment to her unborn baby is the making of a promise, assuring her bond to an infant whose survival depends on her care. This lens was no use to me. My attachment to Gabriel was not the beginning of something else; it was happening now, before he was born. It was a promise being kept in the making. And in the same way, surely, even in the oxygen-deprived, sleepy, incomplete, possibly unconscious mind, even if the activity of the brain was more physical than cerebral, surely something was being made that counted now and not only for later. I wanted an underwater lens that pressed against him, that would move with him as he grew, that would feel the feelings of the unborn mind to understand how his promises are experienced in the making, that would tell me if there was wonder, fear, pleasure, the dark impression of something gathering. These studies could tell me no such thing.

If the things I sent to him made any contri-bution to his forming mind, it must have been modest, attenuated as it was by the tissue between us and the hormones that subdued him. And if they reached him, they would not have made his world more full, more rich, more present to him than it

might otherwise have been, much as I wanted this
to be true. It was most likely that the breadth and
depth of his experience were no greater with my
care than they would have been without. It was
just possible, though, that whatever he received
from me made his life *differently* rich than it might
otherwise have been, and different in the direction
of the cadences of our family life. So I sent these
things to him, aware neither I nor even he would
ever know what use he made of them, what dear
muddy assemblages he would leave on the sand
to be washed away by the shattering tide of his
birth, but I felt that the more I sent him, the closer
he might build himself to us. I allowed myself to
imagine that perhaps there was a kind of pleasure
in invention for him as there was for me; or if not
pleasure exactly, then at least a kind of neural
reach, an exertion all his own, that would remain
forever private to himself.

As his mother, coming to terms with this possibility struck me as the greatest letting-go, as though
he were leaving home all grown-up and no longer
would I know what he was doing. The prospect
of his independence from me was unthinkably
sad, and it was thrilling. In these private cerebral
exertions Gabriel could not be a figment of my

imagination, nor even a function of his own gestation. He was making a world all his own; and all the more his own because it would never come true to us. An expanse of possibility lay before him. There wasn't much time, and there wasn't much of him to use it, but perhaps it was real.

While he prepared to leave home, and I prepared for the complication of his birth, these furthest depths of hope and poetry and science offered little consolation for what was to come. None of it was certain. All that was fixed and sure was the slender promise that I would, I certainly would, one day soon hold him in my arms and kiss him every inch – although in the end, when it was time, I forgot to grant these kisses.

FOUR

Around this time we learned there was a very small chance Gabriel could survive more than a few hours and into another day, and so a nurse from the children's hospice came to our house to meet me in advance. The woman who arrived seemed to be such a normal person. She gave me half a hug by way of a greeting. Over the other arm hung a cardigan and a roomy handbag with a plastic folder sticking out. I made us each a cup of tea and we went to sit together on the sofa, side by side. It was morning and the sun was coming through the open window to lay rhythmical slants on the opposite wall, lending the room a feeling of brightness, optimism, almost festivity on the day that someone had come all the way here, almost an hour's drive, just to talk about Gabriel. By now it was November, and with Anatole back at nursery the house was quiet. His downstairs toys were thrown into big felt boxes either side of the fireplace: one for train track, one for animals and one for Lego, the Lego box pushed out of shape by a wide farmyard he had built the day before and told me not to take apart. A row of multicoloured books filled a shelf above the radiator, spines exposed and curling on the ones he read the most.

I thanked her for coming, and the thank you contained an expression somewhere between surprise and apology that she had made the journey for such a marginal case. It was an attempt to express an unclear feeling that ours could not belong among the unthinkably sad stories of the hospice. There was nowhere it could belong, this half-mythical story. It was happening privately, inside my own body, and surely for the first time in history. Like when you fall in love and believe no one in the world has ever felt as you do, there couldn't be other stories like ours. Nor could there be a dedicated building, just under an hour away, with staff who were normal people, and plastic folders ready. Surely she was looking at it all the wrong way. But the best I could explain, casting my eyes around the room for clarity, was that I thought it would have been sadder for us, and more deeming of a place in the hospice, if we had got used to having Gabriel around the house, and he had touched the things we have here and then left them behind.

All the same, we needed things to be left behind. Safe things, symbolic things, markers in the ground whose meanings we could, to some extent, control. When I asked her about coffins and warm shrouds to suit a baby I joked that I was nesting, but we both knew I wasn't really joking. It was true. How many hours I had spent preparing for Anatole, pairing tiny socks and putting them beside a stack of little vests too small to fold, pinning white paper clouds to make a mobile, pressing down a blanket on an empty cot. How peacefully I would lean at the doorway, watching the expectant room. It's like playing with dolls, I said to my mother on the phone. I used to do this when I was little.

Nesting – when the lethargy of late pregnancy lets in peaks of energy spent anticipating the needs of the baby – is practical work that needs doing, and it is imaginative work too. You imagine what it will be like when the baby is here. You let your mind go slow, you go through the motions, you imagine the sleeplessness and set things out for the person you will soon become, whose time is no longer her own. For now, while you still have time, laying hands on the baby's things forces an understanding that soon, though it seems impossible, there will really be a baby in the house. But for us it was also for afterwards, for after he was buried and his reality would be unclear again, to force an understanding that, impossible as it may come to seem, a baby had been here. In these ways ordinary things took on disproportionate importance, and perhaps, compared to a normal pregnancy, nesting brought me disproportionate comfort.

So I went about preparing in the same way I had for his brother, writing lists and ticking things off. Sometimes at the top of a list I would put his name, handwritten neatly and underlined: *Gabriel*. I know the straitened pleasure it would have given me, writing his name and underlining it. Around this time I had sent off for name tapes with his full name on, in blue serif capitals like the ones I had sewn into his brother's school clothes. They would stay in a bundle in a drawer, but I wanted to seed the house with things like these. I wanted a future in which I kept coming upon these things, unexpected reminders, loving and delicately edged in rage: *Our child was real.*

*

December came, and the day before his Christmas play I took Anatole to nursery carrying the costume I had just finished making, with cardboard branches stapled around a fabric collar to give the effect of a snowflake. He had been learning a delicate dance and performing it by the kitchen table, spinning slowly and carefully, soft fingers raised with the beginnings of grace, and then lowering himself to the floor to point his toes very sharply. The children in his group would be performing this dance in pairs, holding hands, all of them dressed as falling snow.

From nursery I drove to the hospital for an appointment they had booked the night before, fitting me in at short notice, as they always managed to do. When I presented my maternity file the receptionist led me to a private waiting room, as she always did, where the other pregnant women were out of sight. Gabriel had sent a ribbon of blood, and although it was too early, they thought he would be born very soon. Whatever he had been constructing, he would have to come away from it now. I thought of Anatole with his Lego, assembling some structure he must perfect, and how reluctantly he puts down his blocks and gets to his feet when we call him away. I imagined all the strange little structures Gabriel had been perfecting in the warmth of his body and mind, and then something calling him away, and reluctantly he leaves them. It was time he was drawn to the surface, poor thing. Some private agreement had been made between my body and his, and now we prepared to receive him.

Watching the sun make its rectangle on the wall of the waiting room, I remembered the bright November morning with the nurse from the hospice, and only now understood the unclear feeling of apology and surprise with which I had met her. It had been the first time someone had approached Gabriel from the other end of his life – meeting him, so to speak, as a child dying rather than a baby forming. She seemed to be able to see him clearly from there, and I could not. I had fiercely resisted the perspective of the medical articles that looked at pregnancy through the lens of its completion in birth and life, but this was her perspective too, and all of a sudden she was right. The effort spent trying to steer the course of my imagination away from his future and into his present had been all-consuming, and now all these efforts needed tipping on their side, very quickly.

By now there were so many of us. Our family, the midwives, the consultants and geneticists of three hospitals, the hospice nurse. Were we all now tipping our efforts on their side? Whatever we were doing certainly seemed to be getting more urgent, but I couldn't pin down exactly what it was we were doing. Had I been keeping the baby in my imagination after all, and now we were trying the alchemy of making him real? Did we think that if we were careful enough and graceful enough, we could make an incision in the surface of my dream so fine that we could slip him through unnoticed, and I would wake from sleep with its treasure in my arms? Surely this was madness, this most unrealistic and ambitious feat of engineering, and yet we were embarking upon it, together, like a kind of shared delirium.

In fact what was coming would be the simplest and most uncomplicated thing. Not even a feat of medical science. Indeed, the part of the doctors in this communal madness was to retreat. I was collected from the waiting room by a midwife who was by now familiar. A scan revealed that Gabriel was alive, but the blood and the contractions I described confirmed their expectation that birth was imminent. The consultant proposed that we did not monitor him during birth. It is normal to measure the heart rate of a baby through the mother's skin so early interventions can be made if it shows distress, but Gabriel's readings might have tripped hospital protocol and sent us to theatre for interventions certain to fail. I agreed. There would be no limit to the care they would provide us, but they would not monitor him, only me.

So they rowed back their boats, oars very quiet in the water, not wanting to disturb the calm. There was the clear impression that they were retreating from something precariously balanced; that this needed to be a perfect performance, our one chance, and they knew better than to intervene. We would all trust our two bodies to do their best, perhaps because it would give him the best chance of being born alive; perhaps because there was nothing to be done anyway. It would be a couple of days, no more.

This was the very end of pregnancy.

I was on my own, not afraid, not abandoned but prepared, honoured, eyes thick and dull with purpose. I drove home. All the arrangements had been made by now, all the lists complete, and whatever had yet to be done no longer needed doing.

A week before, I had had the briefest of dreams. We were burying Gabriel, and the undertaker said it would be simpler and less costly if I were buried at the same time. There seemed to be some catch to his logic but I couldn't bring it to mind. I hesitated – I did hesitate – then I climbed into the grave. When I woke, it was a few moments before undertaker's logic dissolved. It was becoming clear that what Anatole most struggled to understand was no less confusing for me. Was this baby coming or going? Was I giving birth to him or digging him up? Which was it first, womb or soil? The difference felt increasingly unclear. The coincidence of his name did not help. At nursery there was so much talk of the birth of the baby Jesus and the shimmering visit of the Angel Gabriel, messenger of good news. The baby, taking mortal flesh like us to briefly touch our paltry things. The soil, the heavens, the holy visitation. I realized I was preparing for Gabriel's birth as though it were his return to life from the dead, or a visit from the deep or from on high, he who takes away the sins of the world. What story were we in?

The day after the hospital was the nativity play. Onto the low stage stepped Anatole and his friends all dressed as snow. The angel descended from the ocean of heaven, and the baby was released from immortality to lie in the arms of its mother, and the snow fell, rejoicing from its fingertips to its sharply pointed toes.

That afternoon, back home from the play, I gathered the blankets that would be Gabriel's and put them into the washing machine. Two small cotton blankets, barely touched since Anatole was newborn, one for the labour ward and one for burial. One for warm and one for cold. What a relief it was to handle these very simple things. Tomorrow they would be sacred, but for now they were just cotton blankets, the right size for a baby, spinning.

*

On the evening of the last day, I wrote:

You're coming soon, everyone thinks so. I think so too.

It's sad. And it's also a relief.

By the time the blankets were dry I had written to my mother and my sister to say we would need them. The sun rose, a neighbour took Anatole to nursery, and it was my mother, in the end, who drove us to the labour ward. In the car I began to withdraw, my words rolled back into their sockets, and I sank into the night.

The books on giving birth would go unread, and all the better. Four years earlier I had absorbed their advice about labouring in the dark, at night or with eyes closed, shielded from the light of day and lost to the firm ground of lucid thought. Let go, they read – as you do when you fall into sleep, only you are not falling. You are feeling your way, and it is the abandonment of everything else that lets you feel your way most keenly. A strange darkness washes over the mind as labour begins, sending ever-greater waves of chemical sea barrelling over the neocortical infrastructure until all is submerged and quiet. This is how I imagined it. I imagined the sea alive with sensation, teeming with sensors like tiny medusae making the water thick with their number, each one a lens bending and glinting on tides of feeling so the whole sea was an instrument of fluid perception. There will be pain but do not be afraid, they wrote. Let yourself go under. Endure it, because soon your baby will be here. Be flooded by the rivers of hormones and they will carry you to the other side: oxytocin for love and uterine contraction, beta-endorphin for pain relief and the euphoric bonding of mother and child, prolactin for milk, catecholamines for clearing the baby's lungs.

These books, retrieved from our shelves in the first weeks of this second pregnancy for pleasurable reading in bed, were moved after a few months to the floor underneath the bedside chair, and later returned to their shelves unopened. They seemed so naive to me, these books, so swept up in the tides of expectation, that they failed to notice the darkest part of the night, the navel of the dream, which was death.

FIVE

I open my eyes. The gloved hands of the midwife have hold of a new bright red thing which, in a single arching swoop, she is delivering to my arms. What must have been barely a second spans minutes in my memory. The smooth arc of her movement is complicated by a completely independent project of twists and little stretches this red thing is embarked upon: the first news he is alive. In the muscular squirming of his form I can read the sensation of his birth made flesh. He gives substance to the sweet tug of that remarkable unjointing, that tender dislocating of him from me and the closing up of my internal organs to regain the space he took up, the roar of sorrow and exertion pushed from my lungs: all these sensations are somehow gathered into the shape of him so that everything is one. I take him in, this dazzling slippery star, somehow in flight; I take in the single moment of his life not spent pressed against the fluid warmth of his mother – and now, how silently, he is collapsed upon me, exhausted, resting, like a vital organ removed and laid on my chest for comfort, and here: he is back in his lake of me.

Suddenly there is time, and nothing and everything to do.

We say hello to this baby. We speak to him. We tell him he is just right, just as he is. Hello, hello, we say to him. He is all treacly; so is my hand which holds him wet and secret under the blankets put around us. He feels so strong and rounded and lovely, secure and fat and complete. I am almost surprised to find he is a real baby.

For months we had been attending his growth on greyscale monitors in the darkened rooms of specialist clinics, and for these months he had been transparent. We could see through him. When the sonographer increased the pressure against my skin we could move through him and out the other side, as though one of us, or both, were ghosts. We had watched the cursor deftly dropping markers at his outlines to measure head circumference, femur length, the distention of his bowel, the depletion of amniotic fluid. We knew the size of his lungs in relation to the cavity of his chest, the anatomy of his heart, the mouse-quick beat of his pulse, and we had often toured the organs of his face, even though these had nothing to add to the diagnosis, and when it appeared on the screen it had usually been as a gift to us, to let us see him. In the busy hospital schedule these gifts were offered as briskly as kindness would allow, and they were always unrewarding. We wanted to see his face but we didn't mean this – the strange broken outline of a profile interrupted by the nasal cavity, the mouth a jagged cut reaching back into the throat between glowing hooks of white – we meant the soft plains you could imagine kissing.

Now, heavy against my chest, this apparition is turned real and there are no outlines at all. Being real, and not transparent, and not a cross-section of himself, his interior has become his own at last, and he tends to himself with the otherworldly wisdom of the newborn, his whole body an instrument of sensation, eyes closed tight as if to keenly feel his way. Here is our baby son. His face is crumpled into a dear little scowl. A fan of grumpy fingers, skin too loose, mutely probes the space around them. When his father touches a giant forefinger to his tiny palm it is softly gripped. We begin to make out his face, a little like his brother's and a little his own. He is so quiet and small that if you cast your eye over the room you wouldn't know he was here at all.

But he is here, and the little flexions of his fingers and the fluttering of his heart are enough. They are more than enough. They are announcements that extend just beyond the limits of his body to the grown-ups who surround him, and quietly, not wanting to disturb him, we amplify them. His father sends a message to his sister, at home with our little boy. One midwife whispers to another, who leaves the room.

Further away from the baby, the announcements he set in motion move faster and with more noise. In the office of the labour ward the chaplaincy register is consulted and a Catholic priest urgently called. He is out on some business and will rush to the cathedral to gather a candle and oil, get ready the shortest form of the baptismal rite, get in his car. Anatole, one day shot of his nativity play and with the song of the Three Kings always on his lips, is told the long-awaited words: Gabriel is here. He will put down his toys, move swiftly and wordlessly through the house and out of the door, arms helped through the sleeves of his coat. Arriving at the hospital he will rush towards the heavy double doors, where some private thought will stop him for a moment, he will pause, he will pause – and then go on. In her car my sister will reach the end of a long journey from her two young sons to mine. And my mother, who had driven us to the hospital with tears in her eyes, will have found a parking space and made her way back to find, in the space of only minutes, this grandson breathing in her daughter's arms.

So there is the movement of people arriving. Mother, sister, sister, son; the priest not yet. They move in formations around the bed, voices floating, eyes wet, rejoicing. The little boy comes closest, wide-mouthed with relief, and kisses us. Somebody thinks to take a photo of the four of us together.

By now I am sleepy. I have fused into a kind of dream with our baby, if a dream can be made of body as much as mind. His little breaths rise and fall on the waves of my lungs as though we are sealed together, as though you could press a sonographer's wand against the surface of our dream and find a single shared interior, our organs mixed, outlines transparent, a miracle of synchrony. Nothing is the matter now. We are settling in, and there will be nothing else. I will wait with him until our lovely, complicated self depletes and simplifies into those who are living and those who aren't.

Yet I am wrong.

Unmistakably, he is inventing something of his own. He is inventing the crumpling of an eyelid, and with this crumpling, a little black crescent of sight breaches the surface of our dream. Almost as soon as it opens it closes again, and I am left in wonder.

What did he make of this, his sip of sight? It looked effortful, and I wonder if it was. I wonder if this little push was his greatest adventure in defiance of death, like the furthest leap of a fish, the gleaming curve of its back above the waves just enough to let slip a darting swooping secret life beneath. I wonder if it was a glimpse of effort and pleasure and something like the joy of being alive. If it was, I hope his effort was repaid with equal force. I hope it felt, to him, like the opening up of his whole self, opening the floodgates onto all the world, onto a great tumbling and crashing of world without end – far, far into the skies above the river and the hills and all the land, the very curve of the horizon, all the creatures, all of us – and I hope he sipped of it before his eyes were sealed. Then between womb and soil there would have been time, just, for him to stop and look around. And I hope he saw me watching, and something was imprinted in his mind then.

*

The curtain is drawn back on its rail and a woman in scrubs announces the arrival of the priest. Different things matter suddenly. My body is covered. The midwives demote themselves to the foot of the bed. Gabriel stays the same, eyes closed again, monitoring himself.

The priest brings another kind of hush into the room. His long black vestments are out of place in the maternity ward, where things should be noisy and bright and opening into life, yet this is the hush he brings. He has come to gather the moment. Life has its formalities, and here is Gabriel's. There wouldn't be birthdays, school days, leaving home all grown-up, but there was this, and in this moment it felt like plenty. The priest was a different kind of creature from the people we had become since Gabriel was born. We had grown from Gabriel, and he had grown from something else. He seemed to move at a different speed; not faster or slower but as though he were set to a different time, from which he was able to bring the whole world and its history into the room just for a moment, all for this barely born child.

Now he was here he did not rush. He was courageous from the very beginning, just like our midwife. Like her, he knew the work he had to do, he knew there was a hurry, and that it couldn't be hurried very much. He asked our names and Gabriel's especially. What a sight we must have been, so many figures stationed around the baby, settled in as though this room were our home now and we would gladly never leave. How proudly we pronounced his name in full. How proudly we showed him this wonder of a child. There was a little time for admiration. A Catholic godparent was sought and found in Anton's sister Susanne, standing at the foot of the bed with my sister and the midwives, she who had helped Anatole from his Lego and into the sleeves of his coat and brought him to us. These were the preparations, and then he set out his instruments on the round-edged surface of the bedside table, and began the liturgy of the rite of water.

In the weeks before Gabriel's birth I had looked up the words and gestures of the baptism and their significance, to try and understand what they might mean for the faithless mother of a Catholic child. I read about the ancient gods Yahweh and Elohim, and all the legends of water and flood and salvation that flow into the pages of the Bible and convene upon the ritual of baptism that cleanses with water symbolic of new life. On different pages I read that there was a word for the underwater feeling newborn babies are meant to feel, all at sea in their mother's arms. People call it *oceanic*: the peace of oneness with the infant's world that is the loving mother. A century ago it was thought that this first underwater oneness might be the source of all religious feeling: a feeling that once, before life really began, far back in our bodies' histories, there was this oneness we always miss thereafter. Perhaps this very feeling, this longing to return, had infused the writing of those early stories that made their way into the water of the Bible and was returned to its source every time a baby as new as Gabriel is baptized, holy water poured back into the oceanic dream that set it going. I had heard of this longing before. Dante called it love, a force which to his medieval mind was a pull almost like gravity: a pull of love towards God and the order of His creation, strong enough even to pull the planets into orbit.

To me it all convened to mean that when you're in the ocean of your mother's arms nothing pulls you. You are, too briefly, exactly where all the forces of gravity would have you be. It isn't for long that nothing pulls you. You surface from the dream soon enough, even if you spend the rest of your life longing to return. And perhaps for Gabriel, that brief opening of an eye had been the beginning of his dream's end, cutting into the darkness with a sliver of brightness so dazzling it might have frightened him. I wonder if he felt it like a cut, a blade, a searing noise that pierced him. What an adventure, that cut. So newly born, his senses would have been all muddled, and sight might well have felt like sound or smell or touch, and he might have felt himself and me and all the world to be a single breathing self. A lovely self, I hope.

But we don't really know what he felt. Apart from the stethoscope warmed against the hand of the midwife and pressed to his chest sometimes, Gabriel was not monitored as he lay in my arms, and even if he had been, there would have been little gained. For all the transparency of our organs laid bare to the probes that had brought us safely to this point, those assemblages collecting on the shore of his mind would remain obscure to science.

There are always other instruments, though. If the instruments of science have been honed over the years, so too have the instruments of the imagination: traditions of thought finely sculpted by the passage of time and keenly sharpened by the words of poets and mystics and priests. Maybe Rilke had the measure of his world.

A few years before, Anton had spent weeks translating Rilke's 'Eighth Elegy', getting the flow of meaning and the strangeness of the syntax right, and I had pored over his translation and all the little turns between the lines. I loved the poem for the way it imagines the peaceful silence of the animals who move about not feeling themselves to be distinct from the world around them. They eat of the world, and they are of the world, and when their remains are returned to the earth perhaps the oneness of death is not so different from the oneness of life. Back then, Anton and I didn't know that the turn between lines six and seven would contain the life of our second son: a fraction of a phrase that dwells upon the perfect oneness with the world of newborn sight that sees no patterns and knows no place among them. The poem is a lament, and it is the loss of this oneness that it mourns.

Blankets wrapped across me, I attended the baptism as I had attended the antenatal scans that would no longer visit my body: listening, watching, understanding not much but knowing there was expertise in the room. The doctors, the scholars, the poets, the priest: each had seemed to drift into view just when they were needed, each bringing just the precision we looked for at each station of Gabriel's life. Swept along by currents of oxytocin and beta-endorphin, I believed all these people existed because of love, tending to our boat with care passed down through generations. All of human wisdom bound up with craft and passed through the inks of the liturgical texts read and translated over and over, through the pages of medical journals and training manuals and drawn to us time and again as if by gravity to tend to us with these acts of love. My sister and I looked at one another with round eyes. Both of the midwives were weeping. At this time, to weep was exactly the expertise they brought. These women knew birth and how ungathered and noisy it should be, and what they offered was their sorrow. The room was warm with candlelight.

Only afterwards did I reflect that the baptismal candle had never been lit, such are the regulations of the hospital wards. The congregation of us, the hallowed baby in my arms, the midwives weeping, the rhythm of words: these must have been enough to make the light soft.

SIX

The light stayed soft for a while after the priest left, and perhaps the rhythm of the liturgy had moved to the people around the bed, because their voices and small movements seemed to cradle me as I lay half-sleeping, and perhaps they cradled Gabriel too. Here was family life, Gabriel just another one of us, taking his place easily among our number. It was during a conversation between Anatole and a kindly doctor about his nursery that the midwife pressed her stethoscope to Gabriel's heart and heard no sound.

She met my eyes without a word and I remember I nodded. In that moment, I remember I felt the news of his death to be very small indeed, and that if I could hold it close enough and keep it warm in my arms, it would be a secret safe with me. We had laid him against my skin so my body could regulate his – a miracle of synchrony, I had read – so surely, for a little while at least, one heart between two would be enough. There was still air in my lungs, still sleep in my mind, and surely one sleepy mind was enough to keep us both inside our dream. It was true he would never move again, but if I didn't move either, then surely nothing would need to be different for quite a long time.

Here we were, all our family together, a tableau of figures around the bed each busy with their part. Anatole was describing his nursery Christmas play, and the chocolate button every child had been allowed to eat afterwards because they had each been so good. In my arms was all of the length and weight of his brother. All of his adventure. All he had sipped of the tumbling and crashing of world that was his.

During this secret time I watched Gabriel for any sign of what was becoming of the world he had made. His eyes were so closed. The substance of those thoughts I had imagined him assembling would be wetted and stuck down by now, flat and airless like the gills of a fish out of water. The parts of his body that had been making those thoughts were now as heavy as the parts that were lungs, were bowel, were heart. I wondered how quiet was his chest when the midwife heard no heartbeat.

How long before a body so small falls silent. Surely not so soon. Perhaps she heard something like the sounds of the womb but their opposite: a soft watery jostle of cells relaxing, blood slowing down, organs becoming unfamiliar to themselves, and perhaps, most distant of all, my heartbeat, big and slow like a whale in the sea beneath him.

And perhaps there is never perfect silence, just the exchange of one kind of movement for another, a body no longer in the making but unmaking—

Here was the size of the news. Without a sound our son had turned and begun to go away. Not even to another place but inward, into himself, and we could not follow him. Our dear son. He was gone and he yet was here, concentrating ever more into his body. It was sickly, nightmarish, irreversible, and the people in the room had to be told.

I gave to Anatole the sad honour of the announcement. I didn't want the news to pass among all the adults in a grown-up way as he listened beside his brother. Only a few seconds could have passed before the kindly doctor brought their conversation to a close, perhaps having noticed the wordless exchange between the midwife and me. I said his name and recited words I still remember well, because we had rehearsed together bedtime after bedtime when he pressed his fabric hippo against my tummy and pretended to be the doctor himself: Our midwife has just told me Gabriel's heart has stopped beating, and so now he has died, and now we will begin our strong mixture of feelings.

Of this time there is little more that I remember. I expect Anatole looked at his baby many more times and gave him many more kisses before he was helped back into his coat to go home. Perhaps Anton drew close to his baby and me, perhaps he extended his hand to the little face, perhaps he put his arms around us. Perhaps my mother and our sisters did something like this too. I don't remember, but when somebody dies people must draw close and hold one another and share the last of the warmth. What I do remember was the feeling of all the people and things in the room just slightly lifting and beginning to float, barely perceptibly, from the surfaces they should have been weighted to. A little drift. It was as though the centre that had been holding us was suddenly insubstantial, and the drop in gravity cast everything subtly awry, and gradually loosened the bonds between us until our family found it possible to go back home, and strangers found it possible to come and go almost as though it were normal.

*

In the hours that followed, the warm light that had seemed to surround us grew colder and gradually more dark. I don't remember how long we let Gabriel rest after he died, but by the time we finally moved him all our family had gone home, and only the midwife and Anton and I remained. Now that we wouldn't be bothering him I wanted to see his face properly at last. He felt even more fragile now than he had been when he was alive, and I didn't know how to move him. So together we three lifted him, not far, a handspan away, and laid him beside me on the bed. In my sleepiness I asked the midwife to take a towel and roll it tightly along its length. She followed my instructions without question, and when I asked her to curve the rolled-up towel around Gabriel like the wall of a nest to make sure he wouldn't fall out of bed, she did so. At the time this seemed to me the natural thing to do. It was only afterwards that I realized why: when Anatole was born he too lay on my bed for a little while, and our midwife then had rolled him a nest from a towel. It didn't occur to me that Gabriel needed no such provision, lying so still beside me.

I put my arm around him and held the palm of my hand around the back of his head, so tired that the most lovely prospect in my imagination was to fall asleep holding him. The previous night I had slept very little, if I had slept at all, and now a new night was approaching. But I couldn't sleep.

There came a doctor who regretted that she needed me to complete a form, so I turned onto my back again and was helped to sit up, and a biro was put in my hand. Two women in scrubs stopped at the door and came in to admire the baby. They seemed to know me, and though I couldn't place them I was glad of the admiration. I wanted more people to come and see him. Anyone. I recognized the consultant who had prepared the raft of measures we never needed because he never showed distress. She had seen my name on the whiteboard and wanted to say hello. Another woman, very tall, hair scraped back, brought a clipboard with the autopsy consent form. I was holding Gabriel in my arms again, and there was a moment's deliberation as she hesitated with the clipboard in the air and I transferred the baby to Anton's arms. The neatness of the exchange – a dead baby for his autopsy consent – had all the symmetry of a well-crafted joke; a horror all resolved when she thanked us and said goodbye and that she was sorry for our loss. With these words she became somebody who loved Gabriel too, and whom I could easily love. Still drowsy with feeling, I loved all the people who came to see him.

Now he had died there were so many things to be done, and by so many different people, that the room was seldom quiet again. Every time the door was opened and the curtain drawn aside, the cold and clatter of rooms and offices in the corridors outside were revealed with greater clarity until the dream had almost lifted, and with it the glow of warmth that had held us until now. Perhaps it was just normal life begun again, but I felt it as the tender pulling away of something essential – something like oxygen or love or the roundness of a world with all the noise damped out. Perhaps this feeling came from deep inside me, from something in the death of a baby in its mother's arms that rapidly strips the hormones and begins to cancel the synchrony.

Perhaps the feeling was helped by the little oval pill our midwife had brought me to suppress the production of breast milk. I didn't want to take it. I told her I would, but not yet, and as she left us to ourselves I turned to Anton and we watched the dreadful white pill in its little paper cup. I would have done anything, I said to him. I would have never slept, I would have stayed awake every night to feed him. Yes, he said, you would have done anything.

It tasted bitter, medieval, an old wives' tale of a pill the colour of milk but in every way its opposite, and most of all so dry – dry enough to desiccate all the milk of those silent hours that would have been ours. Without this pill I would overflow with need for him, or worse, would be overfilled with need, breasts swollen thick and engorged with milk undrunk, love unspent, milk he would have loved to receive as my body would have loved to give it. Everything was darkening.

Looking back, I am glad I didn't sleep. I imagine it would have been a leaden sleep so dreamless it would have made my mind go solid too, like Gabriel's, and there would have been no more dream, no more sleep, and I would have died, my body having forced a desperate resolution to the miracle of our synchrony and got it wrong, following him down and down into death instead of coming up for air.

But the alternative frightens me more. Had they let me sleep and I had woken too late, I would have missed the brief and gentle time when he seemed only to be asleep: the hour or less before his sulking cheeks would subtly flush, his face and head would become softly heavier, the features somehow thicker, or just so set in their pose as to seem to have thickened; before the fingernails grew dark; before his lovely mouth darkened and the inner parts of his perfect lips turned deep black. Had I slept – had I slept then, I would have woken to a baby quite lost to death. Instead I stayed awake through the gentle time, death and sleepiness lapping at the bed from all around, and we watched him, and held him, and, in cool water, we bathed him too.

I have a video recording of this time, and I watch it very rarely, as rarely as I open the bag his blue woollen hat is sealed inside, as though looking at the video, like opening the bag, would release his smell and it would go away. It is the only recording of any length we have, and it is a good recording. The floor of the room, the edge of an open cupboard, and the bed moves into view, the translucent plastic bath set upon absorbent sheeting before which I kneel while my husband stands beside me. The midwife is saying sorry that the water must be cold, not warm. I am replying to her, and my husband is already silent, tending his son in the water.

In the water Gabriel is his most perfect, most comfortable, skin most clear, mouth and brow most at rest, legs floppily crossed in memory of the womb. All the loveliness of a baby. For once he just looks asleep. I watch my husband's hands. The heel of one hand rests on the side of the bath and the other works very softly at his son's hair, which we could say we are meant to be washing. A little work at his temple, neatening as if for a proud first day at school, and then his fingertips hold in the water a moment or two, and his other hand visits the legs and little toes, sees if there is cleaning to be done there, then retreats to rest on the side again, soap suds up to his wrist. He lets me. My hands seem to know the baby, the right hand honoured to support his head, thumb stroking his hair, its incidental movement giving the impression of a baby all tired out and nuzzling in his sleep. I pluck his drifting hand from the suds to lay on his chest and it slips back into the water.

Then we dried him, and some hallowed towel made its way to the hospital laundry as we rolled up the sleeves of a tiny white sleepsuit never worn and much too big, one sleeve to each of us, until his right hand could be seen and then his left. Everything we did made the darkness grow.

A different midwife, no less courageous than the first, asked me why we didn't plan to stay the night. By now we knew we would have been allowed to hold him as long as we wished, his little body arranged into poses natural to our sad bodies, and gradually say goodbye. We could have slept all night in a bed beside his cot – his cold cot, as we knew it was called, a chilled unit supporting a Moses basket within which he would be wrapped in blankets, as though to keep warm.

She asked if we were worried about how he might look. I said no, it wasn't that. It was that his body was becoming his own. I tried to explain that we didn't want to stay so long that we made his body ours and began to treat him like a doll, when his body was his own. In fact I said *dolly*. What a strange word, chosen to soften the word *doll*, which seemed too abrupt and cruel a thing to call a baby, though *dolly* had a stranger tone. But everything was strange. I was strange. He was the strangest of all, and becoming stranger.

This is how we knew we had to leave him. When Anatole was a baby I used to put him to my shoulder, pat him on the back and rock him, and from there he would look around. I would turn my back on things to let him observe them. It was his window onto the world, this shoulder-height. I wanted to have held Gabriel like this, just to pretend, just once. So when he was bathed and dressed I gathered the bundle of him in my arms, so familiar a thing to do but so strange, and my arms felt the strangeness, my palm supporting his head as though he were a real baby, and I held him a moment to my shoulder, little cheek against mine, my head leaning towards his. I arranged him in this way, and I pushed back my head and I opened my mouth wide as it would open until the corners nearly split and howled a long, desperate, soundless howl for me and for Anton, these two wild things we had become, quiet and almost composed at a precipice of what a human being can endure.

It can't have been long I held Gabriel there. Not more than a minute, and I think much less. When I brought him down to my chest to see him again the lobe of a tiny ear had been folded against itself, and now it wouldn't easily fold down. And I saw that something in the soft symmetry of his expression had moved very slightly under the pressure of my skin and would not go back. And I was so sorry.

This was plenty to understand that his body had become all his own, and not ours at all. Our need of him was so far in excess of his need for us that it was turning over itself and beginning to curdle. It took from him, depleted him, made him go bad, cut hair that would never grow again, diverted his body from the lovely journey it was embarked upon, back to shore, back into the soil, back into the familiar belly of the ground. We had watched him steer his own solitary boat across the black waters to safety. He had done it by himself. We had put our arms around his little vessel to cradle it best we could, but we could not board, and we could not steer its course.

When the duty consultant had completed her rounds our cold cot was wheeled into the room. We would come back tomorrow to say goodbye, and for now we let him rest, and we went home.

SEVEN

At home, the women were all still awake and I was glad to slip between my mother and sister, curled up with a blanket over the three of us. Everyone was happy. There was something exhausting in the happiness, something darkening and almost black, but for now the relief was great and we were glad. The child had been born, his life momentous, the seventy-two minutes of his span all spent in his mother's arms. It had been a rich life, full and great and heavy with meaning. It had been peaceful. So much had happened during those minutes you could almost call them busy, but they had not been busy. Everything had taken place as though in slow motion, the sounds and movements damped and rendered graceful as though underwater, every movement part of a slow and deliberate dance, a frightening and monstrous dance, laid at last to rest. All evening we stayed

on the tiptoes of our dance and our happiness, too
tired to stop, too tired to look at the blackening
that was on its way.

Before I went to bed I pottered in the kitchen
with my mother getting something sweet to eat.
She told me Anatole had had toast before bed.
What did he have on it, I asked. Marmite and
honey mixed together, she replied with a quizzical
eye. Did he normally have Marmite and honey
mixed together? Never in his life before tonight.
But he knew the mixture from me. I had made it
up months before to answer a distinct wish for salt
and strength of flavour mid-pregnancy. Batting
around in the kitchen, Anatole and Anton would
catch one another's eye to laugh at me for so odd
an innovation. Yuck, they would say. I would take
in their glee, hands on my hips, and stand my
ground. It's fortifying, I would say, crunching. It
makes me strong.

That night we heard a sleeping cry from the
room above ours. I went up, crept past the temporary bed Susanne had laid for herself beside our
son, and collected him in my arms. I carried him
down and we all lay together in the sadness, the
same three who had laid together the night we had
brought him home from the hospital four years

before. Again, a baby had been born, and again, there were three of us in the bed.

*

The following morning I wanted to sew one of Gabriel's name tapes onto the blanket he would be buried in. It seemed to take all morning and most of the afternoon, folding over the ends to make a neat seam, sucking the cotton to get it fine enough to thread, bunching up the blanket over my knees, folding the end of the name tape again. I sewed at the kitchen table where Susanne was making lebkuchen with Anatole in time for Christmas, measuring the spices and nut flour, chopping the fruit, sweeping sticky crumbs from the board with the side of a cupped palm. Anatole in his apron followed her movements closely, never far from her side, helping count out rice paper circles and laying them on baking trays ready for the spoon-fuls of mixture that would spread in the heat and cover each one.

It was getting dark by the time the name tape was ready, and raining heavily. Susanne drove us all to the hospital, dropped off Anton and me at the entrance to the labour ward and set off to find something cheerful nearby. There was a cafe she hoped would be open, and despite the bitter cold perhaps she and Anatole would have an ice cream each, even a chocolate one, and read some of his books together.

We ran through the puddles with the blanket held under my raincoat. I thought strongly that it might fall into the black wet on the ground, but it did not. At the reception desk we had been expected. There was a plastic folder put aside for us with some paperwork ill-suited to the occasion: a coloured flow chart tracking post-partum early warning signs, and instructions on how to register a birth and death. It was a little while before we were collected, and I imagined what would have been happening. The cot selected from a cold clean room, name and numbers checked, wheeled through hopefully empty corridors so as not to distress anyone who might see it. The rectangular lid removed once inside the room and the midwife viewing the baby: a sorry sight, she must have thought, a baby dead, and looking dead, and this is what I must present to them. This was all they could long to see, the man and woman sad in the waiting room, hunched on their chairs, leaning against one another with hands held tight, far beyond words.

*

We were led through these unlit corridors further and further from the sounds of women giving birth and their babies' early cries, towards a room held secret for the families who tend to babies dying and dead. We had visited this room some months before to prepare for what was to come, and on that ordinary day the corridors did not slope precipitously downwards towards a room deep, deep underground, as they seemed to this evening. The door she unlocked revealed a room so thick with sorrow our limbs moved only slowly. It was almost imaginary there. Not a frightening place, not unsafe, but not real either. It was not real that the floor and walls and ceiling all sloped down towards Gabriel's cot, and that by following this sloping we found him. It was not real that his cot was the only thing in the room, and the only few feet of space not in darkness. But our son was here, this much was real and true, and we found that by moving our limbs we were able to keep our balance as we proceeded along the floor towards him.

The infant we saw before us presented a perfection I had never before experienced. He was so detailed. Certain details seemed to give shape to certain dark corners of the inarticulate loss I felt, so that the sight of him brought relief. He was both very still and very small, even smaller than he had seemed the day before, as though a sculpted miniature had been produced for our comfort overnight. But he was less substantial than a sculpture. He was, by now, a sight. Strangely, since it was the only thing he had not lost, our baby seemed to have lost his corporeality. He was no longer the kind of thing you could touch. Yesterday his whole consistency had been touch and his whole world closeness, and tonight there was no closeness to be found, just sight from afar. Yet from this distance he drew my sight towards himself with such great force I believed this to be the first time I had ever really seen him. If this was sight – this sharpest and most piercing clarity that fixes what is outside into the very flesh of me – then I had never truly seen anything before in my life. And never less so than the day before, when for all our desperate looking and searching and clipping of hair, something about Gabriel had resisted being seen. He had been changing so much he had never really settled, his poor body first getting used to having been born, then getting used to the air and the thinning of breath and then getting used to having died, and all the swift changes it brought. In the hours after his death all our efforts had been directed to this one thing: trying to see him so firmly and finally that the memory might stay with us forever as a child always should, but until this moment he had never yielded to my sight.

Now here he was. Brow no longer furrowed but for the slightest shade of thought still marked, little nose snub and mouth agape, the quirk of an upturned lip that would have broken into the brilliant wide smile of his brother. Like his brother and father a soft fullness beneath the eyes as though tearful or overtired, and eyelids closed so lightly. Everything in miniature. People say the dead look peaceful. Gabriel looked familiar, serious, complete. And then a little hand had been posed where the blanket was folded as if to grip it, to give the impression of a baby asleep. Perhaps the midwife had arranged him thus in desperation, not wanting to present us with a baby so dead, but she needn't have worried. It wasn't being alive that made us love him. Dying had been Gabriel's way since the very beginning, and here he was all grown-up and left home, I want to say, or safely ashore having rowed his little boat all the way across, further than Anton or I had ever travelled. I suppose this is to say that in the composure of his body, in his completeness and resolve, I was proud of him.

Again here we were with our baby, and again there was everything and nothing to do, only this time it was closer to nothing. We must have said things to one another or to Gabriel, though I don't remember what. I remember we stood not quite close to the cot, not quite apart from it, not knowing how to begin to move a baby so resolutely still. Perhaps we wouldn't have dared had I not wanted so much to take from him one last thing, his blanket, and give him ours in return.

Picking him up needed planning. Anton would fold the blanket from home along its width and lay it on the bed. I would stand between the cot and the bed and unwrap the cold blanket from around the baby and, with one hand underneath his bottom and one supporting his shoulders and head, I would lift him in my two hands and turn my body until I was facing the bed, lay him along the vertical fold of his new blanket and there we could relax, and make the next part of the plan.

Gabriel's skin was very cold. His little cotton suit was very cold. It wasn't just the cold of the absence of warmth, but of the silent refrigeration unit fitted beneath the basket they had laid him in. When I lifted him there was an uncanny flatness and lightness. He was somehow papery, as though he might almost rustle. This is the sensation of touching a thing that is now absolutely a sight, no longer to have or to hold, only to see. We were here as though in error, two parents left over past the end of their son, wanting to touch what is not touchable. This had to be as far as our error would go. Just the blanket, then nothing more. I held this sight in my arms and I turned to the bed. Perhaps his hair would have been curly like mine. When I laid him on his blanket on the bed it was familiar, as though we were going to change his nappy. We said sorry to him, and that we would only do this one last thing then let him rest. There was no nappy to be changed, just our blanket folded around him and then another cautious collecting of the body into my arms. I remember that I wanted to have rocked him in my arms, and between the bed and the cot I tried, but the rocking never really took. I laid him down, both hands inside the blanket and little face exposed, and we loosely tucked in the sides. We could not believe how lovely he looked. His tiny, tiny nose, that little brow, eyelids wet with my tears.

It was not possible to kiss him for the last time. Anton and I attended one another like the last ones left of a species, holding one another, watching one another, eyes empty and alert. By now we had sent for Susanne to collect us and she was waiting in the car park with Anatole, and yet it was not possible. There was still everything to do, and there was no time left. Perhaps time passed and perhaps it didn't. When I turned from the cot I found that Anton, without a word, had closed the door behind him, leaving me the honour of the last goodbye.

I saw, too late, that I needed to leave something with Gabriel. A blessing, a promise, something of the one who had carried him, but there was nothing ready – no liturgy, no oil, no ritual. I laid my hands on the blanket that covered him, and pressed my mouth on his forehead, and kissed. I spoke some ordinary words left over from a dream I had had while he was still alive, a dream of saying goodbye and thick, thick snow and notes passed under a door. With these words I lifted my hands from his blanket and my mouth from his forehead carefully, as though I had balanced something there, as though something had stayed. If I blessed him, it was in this lifting away and his stillness thereafter. This was the completing I could give him.

The cold of his face stayed on mine for as long as I could let it. I shut the door behind me. It was not possible, and yet it was done.

*

The rain was bright as darkness outside. I ran to the car, Gabriel's blanket gripped under my raincoat like illicit spoils. I was wearing the brightly patterned cotton skirt Anatole had loved the previous summer for the dark pinks and soft greens of the flowers, and in the rain the flowers wetted and the fabric stuck together. Wet and cold in the car I wanted the cold to stay, the cold, cold face so smooth, the bitter silence. If I could press my arm against the door, my forehead against the chill of the window, then the glass and its rivers of rain would make it stay a bit longer. Nothing could matter as much as the lovely cold – and yet: here was Susanne putting the car into reverse full of cheer and levity I tried to ignore but could not, such was her insistence, and Anton's insistence too, had they no heart – and then I understood why.

Anatole was in his own emergency. His brother had died and his parents had torn away from him through the rain into the very hospital that had taken the baby and he urgently needed us back – all three of us if he could, the baby too. Later Susanne told me he had shouted in a moment of panic, mouth wet and desperate, Baby *live*, baby *live*. There had been nowhere open for ice cream. They had made a kind of picnic in the car and worked through his storybooks, rain trapping them in, and now it was time to go home.

EIGHT

The first days after Gabriel died there was a new simplicity in the house, as though it were a landscape with nothing up close, no detail, only distant forms on the horizon that moved, if they moved at all, in geological time. They were the forms of love, of being alive or being dead, of being tired or being asleep. In a docile way I could follow with my mind's eye the contours of those distant forms and understand we were part of them too: that all the world, not only the horizon, was made of this simple stuff. The simplicity we felt was just these faraway forms up close, more dense and concentrated than we were used to.

I thought of this time as *grace*. The word occurred to me and I looked it up: grace is said to be a gift, unasked for and yet given. But it was tiring, residing in grace. It took extra energy we didn't have and couldn't help depleting. We were still on tiptoes, still in a dance, overwhelmed by the exhausting beauty of a landscape we dared not tear our eyes from, knowing the blackness was all around us, lapping at our toes.

We took it in turns to sleep and cry and play with Anatole. Three days passed before we realized he hadn't been outside, and we went about putting his bike into the car, easing one of the headrests from its setting, pressing down the seat against its own upholstery, turning the handlebars into the crook of themselves and curving them into the boot. We drove to a playground which, before Gabriel, had always had a patch of tarmac with an arrangement of child-sized roads, pedestrian crossings, roundabouts, turnings marked in playground paint for children imagining they were grown-ups, imagining their bikes and scooters were cars and they were driving to grown-up places, meetings, emergencies, adventures, with grown-up things on their minds. By the time we arrived it was getting dark. The markings on the tarmac were still there; of course they were.

I stayed in the car as Anton carried the bike down the grass slope to the tarmac, holding the hand of his son, and set it down on the pretend road. Because Anatole has never had a brother or sister for company, his father has grown to be his favourite playmate. From the sidelines I always admire the ways they play, the games they conjure from the sheer repetition of moments, phrases, actions that raise a smile then are set into lexicon, to be called back into play with a word, an announcement, the practised gesture of a hand. They fell into one of their chasing games, Anton running and Anatole careering behind on wheels, some obscure understanding between them governing their direction, speed, when to swerve to a halt. Before long it began to rain, and still they didn't come back to the car. Through the streaming windscreen, hands hugged under my coat to keep them warm, I watched them. I watched Anton running, running, running. I could not guess how it felt for either of them.

On my ring finger now were two wedding bands, the second very narrow indeed. When we were preparing to be married I had chosen the narrow one first, from an old jeweller's on the high street where we used to live. None of the rings they suggested had looked right on my hand, and in the end I chose the narrowest they had as though I hoped it might not even show on my fingers and over the years might almost disappear. We ordered mine and his, much wider, engraved with our names: *ANTON TAMARIN*. When the rings arrived mine looked too thin, and I asked the jeweller if he could melt it down and put the gold towards another ring twice the width. He could, he said. But when the second ring was ready he presented me with two boxes instead of one. He would let us keep the first ring and wouldn't charge for it. It must have been an economy, a ring so thin it wasn't worth the bother of melting down. Perhaps, engraved with our names, he preferred it to go to us, who would doubtless find a way to honour it even if honouring meant putting away in a drawer. How strange it had been, having two wedding rings. A spare in case we needed to marry one another again.

In the end the jeweller had been right: we did find a way to honour it. Six years later I would retrieve the box from its drawer and put it into the hospital bag with the nightdress, the blanket and the new baby clothes. When Gabriel died and I woke from our dream I asked for it and pressed it into his tiny palm, where it stayed until it was time to bathe and dress him. While the midwife prepared the bath Anton retrieved the ring, and he slid it onto my finger to join the other one.

I half smiled, half laughed with the surprise of the gesture and the pleasure of its neatness.

Even in the moment of it, I remembered I had met our first vows with the same half-smile, half-laugh, and then, too, the levity had seemed misplaced. With all the ritual done, the rings and vows and kiss exchanged, the priest had broken into a familiar tone and said, Well, you're married now. I'd laughed the same way then, as though it all meant nothing much. A laugh to mark the pleasure of a certain neatness, with a certain reflective distance from the matter in hand. On the day of our wedding we didn't know what marriage was – a leap of faith – but when we held our silent son we knew. This was our renewal of vows. This, so far at least, was what marriage meant.

The car door clunked open and there was Anatole, ready to climb in. I took his face in my hands to kiss and it was so beguilingly cold that for a moment I had his brother back again. But this face was all out of scale, much too big to sate the grief in my hands.

*

Christmas was a week away. Back home we lit the third candle on our Advent wreath and we each

chose a carol to sing; a tradition from Anton's
childhood that each of us, for our own reasons,
liked to carry on. Anton chose 'Es kommt ein
Schiff, geladen'. We only sang the first two verses,
the ship still heavy with its load and in full sail,
silent through the waters, Love bearing her on.
We didn't sing the ship coming home to shore,
the baby asleep in a manger, born to die and rise
again to eternal life. I chose 'In dulci jubilo' because
I thought it might be happy enough not to be too
sad, the sweet jubilation of the birth. Anatole made
up his own song about lebkuchen and showed us
the actions, waving his two biscuits in the air in
specific ways. Lights low, candles lit, we sang, we
did the actions, the three of us, Anatole so large.
His four years of age unsupported by younger sib-
lings growing after him seemed a kind of illness,
worsening over time and getting grave. We were
all too old. We would light the candles for Advent
and sail on, leaving Gabriel behind. I did not want
to go on and on, further and further and further
away from him forever. Never nearer.

Perhaps, I thought, I could imagine we were
also sailing back towards him. After all, at the
end we would lie together. All our mouths would
softly blacken and it wouldn't disgust us, we who

so love one other. When we had laid him beside me in the hospital bed and I turned to hold my arm around him, his head in my cupped palm, he dead and me hoping to fall asleep: I lay with him then. And in the ground, years apart, I would lie with him again.

I had begun to imagine an ocean, black as the inner parts of his poor mouth, an ocean somehow bisected so the depth could be seen from its edge, and it was so deep, or rather so tall, towering up from the ground before me. It was approaching me, or perhaps I was drawn towards it, and towards the relief I would feel to press myself into it and succumb at last. It would release the pressure on my throat and neck that had become familiar in these days, perhaps because then I would be drowned. But surely, I thought, the ocean was where Gabriel was.

*

That night in bed I relaxed into terror. The blackness was here at last. It finally let go its waves and rushed at me, filling my throat and all my body with the fullness of grief and forcing my limbs to move, impossibly, towards a baby that no longer had any place in the world that I could understand, and so their movement stayed completely still.

I tried to gather to my chest the memory of Gabriel collapsed in my arms, but all I could see was the black gash of sight from his eye, and I could no longer believe it was the furthest leap of a secret joy. It must have been some ordinary thing, some involuntary muscular reflex that meant nothing to him. Not the curved back of a leaping fish at all; instead the tar-black prow of a stricken ship, I imagined, indifferently keeling, breaking the surface upended by the blind luck of physics as it begins its roll to the depths of the sea floor. Some dull, leaden thing. And I would come too. I would sink with the indifferent weight of that vessel and stay down. Or perhaps it had been a trap all along; not even the smooth prow of a sinking ship but the black peak of an underwater mountain, cavernous and vast, unmoving, always there, and only for a moment showing. Only for a moment, but long enough to draw me to it: the crag of a rock I rush to splinter myself against. I had loved him too much.

Heavy against the surface of the bed, with great effort I turned my head to Anton and implored him to tell me how to get the baby back. He didn't know. Maybe Anton was drowning too. He was in heaven, he offered, and unimaginably happy. A baby in heaven. Effortfully I pushed my imagination towards that peaceful idea. I watched the idea from the surface of the bed and tried to understand the ways it could be real, but there was no route through, nothing I could touch to feel my way. I am the other part of Gabriel, I thought, not God. The love is me.

Bloody and dark as I was, I could only understand one way to return to him: to get down into the soil where he stayed, my grave level with his, and wait until my coffin and tissue disintegrated and then hope that shifts and lurches in the soil over hundreds of years would bring me to him, bring me around him, lay him back in the crock of my pelvis, bog bodies finally returned to one another, and there we would embrace. But this was sickly. Surely I could not long for such a graceless thing. And in a crowded graveyard might not strange bones drift into our embrace unbidden, might we not drift apart and not together? Who is to say how bones and soil behave?

And he wasn't yet even in the soil. The reality was sicklier still. He had been opened up in the hospital and closed again – sewn closed,

I supposed – and then driven to the undertakers, where he was waiting above ground, in neither womb nor soil, until Christmas was over and
the church and priests were available again, the
churchwardens back at work and the site of his
grave agreed. We were allowed to visit him in
the mortuary, every day if we wanted to, and we
decided we never would. His body had ceased to
be his own by now. From the moment we left him
in the hospital he was, to us, interred. I formed
a picture in my mind of the undertakers moving
with him in the dark, not quite real themselves
but rather a strange, homely people who had given
up their lives to dwell with the dead underground,
domestic deities used to sickly ways and means
and ready to be appeased with gifts or reverence
or generous thoughts.

They had sent us a letter confirming arrangements for the funeral, the modern, sombre flourish
of a monogram introducing the careful scripting
of what amounted to a story they wanted to tell us
about our son. *Your precious baby son*, it read, who
had *fallen asleep* at the hospital, had been collected
and brought into their care, where he would stay
until the day of the funeral. *Will stay with me* were
the exact words. Their intent was kind, but the

comfort they offered was ghoulish: a baby sewn together and darkly asleep in the care of a woman who stayed with him in the ground.

I phoned her once. I had become more desperate than before, and prepared to ask still more of his body than the autopsy, the clipping of hair, the handling, the rocking, the printing of his hands and feet. In a rush I phoned to ask if it was too late to make plaster casts of his hands and feet as well. By now it was nearly Christmas Eve and we had gone to my parents' house to find ways of marking the time together. I had left a message, and when she phoned back I was on the floor with Anatole pushing cars around a road of masking tape my mother was laying on the carpet ahead of us, carefully pleating the inside curve of each bend to make it smooth. It wasn't too late. She would make the casts that day. And don't worry, she added, we're taking good care of him. Over Christmas we put toys in the cots of all the babies we look after.

That's lovely, I said. Thank you.

I didn't ask her to remove the toys. I didn't say that he is dead and will never play and never had, having only known things graver than toys, principally love and death. I wanted her to like me.

I wanted her to feel well disposed towards me so she would be gentle with our son when she cast him. I had my own story to fulfil: that his body was still precious even though it was firmly dead. My story needed her to be kind to this body, have gentle thoughts as she spent time with it, perhaps even love it, almost, as she had the honour of preparing the little hands and feet for their casts, leaving the alginate to cure, peeling it away and making sure the skin was clean of it again, and filling the impression with liquid plaster. When she disposed of the alginate that had touched him so closely and for so long that it had learned his shape – longer than I had ever watched his little fingers and toes, longer than I had ever kissed them or plied them with my hands – I wanted her to mark its loss. I thought the more she liked me, the more she might like him, and so I thanked her for putting the toys in the cot.

Her letter was twinned with another that had arrived around the same time. They made a pair on the shelf, neither one of them more or less adequate to the task. The second was from the diocese: no note, just a certificate of baptism printed on plain A4, signed twice in biro and stamped off-centre with the seal of the cathedral. Nothing ceremonial, and no mark of condolence because the baptism was for the beginning of life, not for its end. In this letter there was no end in sight. No death, just everlasting life. I felt this letter understood more than I did about the birth and death of a baby, and still more than the letter from the undertaker. It was written upon thousands of years of accumulated thought, each word thick with accretions of meaning layered over time to arrive step by logical step at a baby in heaven, unimaginably happy. By comparison the kindness of the undertaker was new and still nervous of death, still finding its way. It was plain that here on the shelf lay two stories of death that neither disagreed altogether nor were reconcilable, and these two stories dwelled with me in the bed that night with all his other stories: the baby in the soil, the baby still within me, the poor surfaced fish with gills stuck and airless, the Angel Gabriel descending from the ocean of heaven, sharp little pointing toes, and I just wanted to climb into the soil and be his again.

NINE

In the shower the following morning the blackness eased into pity for my strange body. I noticed how dark the nipples had become so Gabriel could find them. The small oval pill had done its work and no milk had come, but still my body seemed to wait for him. I wondered how I could break it to this body that our baby had died, as though it and I together shared the baby and only one of us knew the news. It was natural to me to imagine my mind knew more: that the darkened nipples, the colostrum, the womb crimping when I missed him, the blood still gulping down were the expressions of a body gentle and dumb, ready to care for him, longing for his weight and smell and needing to be tricked by simulations. When my arms would rise to my chest to hold him and feel the emptiness there, I could bundle up his blanket and hold it to my chest, or to my shoulder, and all my limbs would relax and the pressure on my neck would be released for a while. And when the blanket wasn't there my body found other ways to ease its loss. Queuing at the post office one afternoon I noticed my hips and shoulders slightly swaying to rock the armful of parcels I wanted to get into the Christmas post.

But perhaps my body always knew more. When Anton and I first saw that curled-up form kicking off the side of my womb like a little swimmer in the earliest of the ultrasound scans, and were delighted and laughed and loved him even then, perhaps my body already knew. It didn't need the sound spectrum of the womb to be turned into image and presented back to itself to know the fluid was depleting, nor later to know there was none left. It didn't need to watch the silent exchange between the consultant and the registrar when I described the first turning of contractions to know, before I did, that early labour was on its way. *Know* is the wrong word, of course. My body didn't know the news, it *was* the news. In the shower it seemed to me that my body was an altogether simpler and more whole species of thing than I am, I who need to be shown things and explained them before I understand.

Really I was the one who didn't know, who still waited for him, who still needed to be broken the news. I love you too, I would reply when ribbons of blood fell from my womb, just as I had when he used to kick. My body knew otherwise, but in my mind he must have returned to the resting place of my womb and sent me bloodlines from there. One day he sent no more and I thought it was another farewell, then I felt swoop after swoop of blood descend and I was glad. I love you too, I love you too.

And just as I used to sing and sway with him, speak to him and write to him and sent him a hazelnut once, now I planned to send him one last line. The undertaker had explained that because his coffin was so light they would lower it into the ground with lengths of a ribbon I could choose myself if I wished, and bring it with me on the day of the funeral. I chose an undyed ribbon of fibres I thought would disintegrate well in the soil. I kept it beside my bed, knowing it would carry him into his grave, and I wished I could carry him myself. In the ribbon I saw a dull possibility: looped around his box, it would have to stay with him in the soil, and there lay some comfort. I unspooled its length into my arms and tried to kiss it all the way along,

from end to end and on both sides, and pressed
these handfuls of looping, folding ribbon against
the wet of my eyes, held it in my arms, rocked it
at my shoulder. These kisses were another last
hope, sent down to his poor bones to meet them
one day perhaps.

*

Just before I tended the ribbon, I had been putting
Anatole to bed when I began to cry. He noticed
and asked me why, and I told him it was because
we had to bury Gabriel in the morning and I didn't
want to, even though we had to. I want to have
him in the house with us, I said, even though we
can't. Then something happened that was new.

Anatole tried out a new phrase, learned from
us and now offered back, his voice a little nervous,
self-conscious perhaps, and the phrase was, You
know what? He went on: I think— And here he
paused, and I listened, willing him to persevere. In
this replete silence here he was, pushing himself
over the edges of his own ability and into new
means. As I had imagined the synapses in his
brother's mind stretching and exerting themselves
into new unbroached constructions of thought,

now I watched him pushing the limits of his mind
to specialize his brain into the shape of one adept
at grief and consolation. He pressed down his eye-
brows and opened his mouth: It – doesn't matter.
Our faces were pressed together, his wetted with
my tears. He had got used to these tears, and
sometimes put his two thumbs against my eyes,
both eyes at once, to press the wetness away. He
had thought hard and this was his conclusion: a
good conclusion. There were ways for us to believe
it didn't matter.

Should I try to cheer up? I asked.

Yes, he said: thinking about all his tiny parts!

And with this, we laughed together about
Gabriel's tiny nose and his tiny ears and his tiny
fingers and toes. And here we were: he had managed it all by himself, a mother smiling again.
Barely four and such a heavy weight for him to
carry. I didn't know whether it would harm him,
knowing grief so well, but this is the world he has
now, and here he must belong.

I was afraid of the funeral. I didn't know how far
down he would be buried, and I was afraid my knees
would give way and I would collapse when he was
lowered underground. I had to keep correcting the
accidental thought that he was being lowered *back*

into the soil as though he had come from there, and that when he was returned to the soil he would at last be coming home, down, down back into my womb, a thought so mealy and rich and black the idea alone felt like witchcraft at work within me.

I remember once, when Anatole was new, I rose very early and he was still in the cot sleeping beside me. I had been unable to sleep because of strange, unsettled dreams about the sun eclipsing, and wanting to see it but being unable to find the proper cast of the sky, travelling up and down staircases, begging directions from strangers, getting no closer, time running out. Awake, I went down into the kitchen and sure enough, there, through the window over the shrubs, the sun and the moon were at their work. A partial eclipse, the sky unnaturally pale and dark, the garden birds fearful and hidden and quiet. I tried to look and look away. The fingernail crescent was already burning into my eye and I was afraid. They were so far away, engendering something silent and secret and terrifyingly large, long anticipated in the news yet more frightening for having dared come true, and I barefooted in the kitchen, half-asleep, so miniature and stupid and accidentally etched in the eye with its encounter. I cast down my eyes

ashamed and gratefully watched the crescent fade
from the blinks of my vision as I sauntered on the
floorboards, everything half a dream. I think this is
the kind of experience people call *sublime*. A kind
of slow-dawning terror that matched the enormity
of fear with the enormity of fear come true. I went
back upstairs and Anatole was still asleep, and my
eyes took in the warm round of his face, the eyelids
soft, little hands glad to receive my touch. I curled
up on my side, watched the rise and fall of the
blanket over him, dozed, waited for his stretches
to begin and the opening of his eyes.

The car arrived. It was all coming true. A coffin
unnaturally small, the body of a baby, the real baby,
hallowed thing, here outside our house which
was such an ordinary place. There was nothing
we could do but go outside and lock the door as
though it were an ordinary door and climb into
the car. The undertakers greeted us as though they,
and we, were just ordinary people, and they drove
the car along.

*

That bedtime there was no need for the ultrasound
game. Anatole's baby had been buried now, and

this gave him new work to do. In his pyjamas warmed on the radiator, all ready for his story and the three lullabies he always had, he sat up alarmed by some unseen rip in the fabric of a thought. He needed to kiss the baby.

He pressed the palm of his hand fiercely against his mouth and kissed it many times. Each kiss he flung with his palm into the air, arm stretching awkwardly out to the side in the direction of the church. In the hours after the funeral Anton had opened the roof light above Anatole's bed and lifted him up onto his shoulders so he could see, across the winter fields and just beyond a row of darkening trees, the tower of the church that marked the place we laid him. So now he threw these kisses towards that place, and each time he stopped short, trying to correct the fling of his hand somehow and get it to work, each time saying to himself a corrective *no*, because each kiss wasn't quite right and needed trying again. In the end none of the kisses was good enough. Not one could he angle well enough or push strongly enough to reach all the way to his baby.

In the kisses he flung I recognized the desperate lines I tried to send Gabriel – the songs, the hazel-nut, the ribbon into the soil. Watching Anatole,

I saw that like him I'd sent each of my lines with a corrective *no*, expressed silently to myself, because not one was good enough.

I said I would bring him Gabriel's blanket, which smells of him, and he emphatically agreed. And his box, he shouted as I went down the stairs. I collected everything I could find and brought it up in the strange wide memory box the hospital had presented us with, and hungrily he looked at it all: two blankets, a little white sleepsuit to match the one we had dressed him in, two anklets with the date and time of his birth, never worn, a small confection of silk snowdrops on a plastic stalk, a square patch of dark blue knitting I never made sense of, and a little candle in a tin.

He asked if it could all be his, and I said yes, and we bundled everything onto his bed. It was nice for him, having so much. He counted the things: eight. He put the anklets around the legs of his toy monkey, a Christmas present I had wrapped extra specially and which, seeming to intuit my meaning, he had named after his brother. He opened the tin and sniffed the candle and closed it again, wrapped the sleepsuit and the blankets into a bundle and said I must lie down beside his bed. He was the doctor again, but this time there was no need to scan me. Instead he asked my name, and the baby's name, and said now he was going to drive the baby to the church.

There followed a careful re-enactment of the funeral, with his baby monkey wrapped in two blankets and pressed into the memory box with the lid pushed down shut. He laid the silk flowers on the box, pulled open the ribbon that was meant to seal it with a shiny bow and together we carried the box, ribbons hanging, to the imaginary grave on the floor. I stood back and observed the graceful twist of my son's knee and the sideways turn of his ankle as he bent at the hips to lower the box onto the floor. It was an unmistakable posture I had seen only once before in my life, earlier that very day. The undertaker must have practised and perfected these movements to confer dignity upon the sad spectacle of a little box travelling its last, suspended with some skill from lengths of the ribbon they had asked me to choose. Like him, Anatole gathered the ends of the ribbon and artfully dropped them across the belly of the box so they fell in a lonely flourish. We found a jar of copper coins and handed them around to all the guests played by us both, and each guest scattered a few over the box just as we had scattered petals into the ground.

Now he said I must sing a song. I stood, hands clasped, mind completely bereft of music. This morning two tall men had stood and sung us plainsong between the readings and the homily, but I didn't know those songs, and anyway the occasion called for something simpler and more familiar. It was an old verse from my childhood I fell into in the end:

What'll I do
When you are far away
And I am blue
What'll I do.
When I'm alone
With only dreams of you
That won't come true
What'll I do.

Sung low and slow but without much breath, the words didn't travel far from the memory of childhood evenings curled up with my family and the television on. It was the theme song of something we liked watching, an unserious comedy shot through with unspeakable sorrow, it seemed to me, by this sombre lament that opened and closed every episode and suggested unvisited depths in the women it portrayed. To me, the song promised grown-up worlds of longing and loss I had never known, and the safety and sameness of my family around me felt all the warmer and more secure because of it.

I didn't get far with the song. Anatole stretched towards me and softly he pressed his thumbs against my eyelids to check for tears and wipe them away, and I picked him up and carried him back to bed. We tipped everything soft from the box back into his bedclothes and I read his story and sang his lullabies. He said the funeral had been too sad for him, and he didn't like us wearing black. The next funeral we go to, we should wear every colour except black, he said. We shall be bright. I stayed, stroking his hair until he was asleep, blanket tightly gripped.

That night I tugged the blanket from his arms, slowly so it wouldn't wake him. It stretched as he resisted. I lifted his hot little hand to release it and it tumbled, part onto the floor, part into my arms and against my chest. It was my turn to sleep, and I needed the blanket for myself. In the morning he looked for it among his bedclothes, and was surprised to find it among mine when he climbed in still dozy.

A few bedtimes later he got everything ready and embarked upon the re-enactment again: monkey, blankets, box, snowdrops, twist of the knee, ribbon, coins, no song this time. He went through the stations of the ceremony without really meaning them, as if to cross them off and fold them up. He must have been putting the funeral away. Unlike the ultrasound game, which had needed playing every night for weeks, I think in these evenings he had managed to smooth out whatever crease had been troubling him in the memory of that day, because we didn't play the funeral again.

TEN

For ten weeks after Gabriel died, with Anatole back in the rhythm of nursery, we had the house to ourselves. We tore out the kitchen. The cupboards, if we wrenched them, came loose and could be unscrewed and with booted feet plied apart on the floor. Blank white paint took their place. From the ladder where I stood painting, the room was geometrically brand new, with novel slanting parts and juts and gaps I had never noticed or never seen. We made all the walls white except at the end, where three tall black cupboards once stood and now left a cavity, and here we hung heavy wallpaper printed with sticky honeysuckle, thick stems and leaden leaves. We got a tile saw and its wet teeth drilled smooth channels through widths of thick ceramic. The glint of noise at the back of my skull was terrifying, but I could hold the tiles steady against the plastic finger guard and watch the channels proceeding, their rounded ends like pleasing typography, as though the tiles were soft. We put down towels and flattened out bin bags to keep the chalky puddles off the floor, and the wet and grit bled through my trousers as I knelt. Then we dragged inside a drawing board once belonging to my parents, scrubbed it and oiled it and put it up as a table where the honeysuckle was.

There on the table we laid everything that was his. Cards and letters people had sent us that mentioned his name. The last branch of eucalyptus saved from the flowers on his coffin and the hessian bow, misshapen in the rain, that had wrapped them. A length of the ribbon I had kissed. The orders of service left over from his funeral, the porcelain holder my mother had brought from home to hold his baptismal candle on the altar, and the candle itself, burned down no more than the length of the funeral. The slouching casts of his hands and feet, white plaster wrapped in white paper. The letter from the undertaker, the letter from the cathedral, the plastic folder with the antenatal flow chart. Our wristbands and his anklets, the cuttings of hair, his hat and his sponge and their smell sealed in a plastic bag. His name tapes, all but one.

We set the candle in its holder to melt for the duration of this farewell. The eucalyptus I pressed between papers and laid under heavy books. The casts, which always surprised me in their brittle lightness, we handled with reverence and packed away in their own small box, and then we packed away the other things too, each in their own way casts of his life and the space it took up, all of them strange and brittle in their own way too, and all slouching, somehow, without him.

And then Anton went back to work, and here was maternity leave without a baby.

*

The silence of the empty house was very loud, as though the bones of my inner ear had been damaged by overwhelming noise and now its absence was all I could hear, the same shape and size as the sound, but heard in negative. The silence had a centre that was very still – so still, it took up space in the house. It did not have a fixed place but was often with me, close to my chest, pressing against a shoulder, pressing a cheek. This bundle of stillness was like the silence in the way it described precisely the absence of what there should be: an absence of little forced movements, small squirms, reflexes gradually opening out, the quickly resolved startles of sleep. A dense concentration of matter, of sprung potential, had been subtracted, establishing an error in the physics of the house. If you could measure the capacity of the building against the volume of the matter it contained you would think there had been a mistake. You wouldn't believe your instruments could possibly be telling the truth.

This stillness and I moved around the house, affecting the physics of the rooms. On reflection I hesitate to call these places rooms, and the range of objects within them our furniture and our things. It's true that there happened to be floors and walls and stairs, and that I made use of these surfaces as I moved through the building, but it was as though the floors and walls and stairs and I were all pretending: pretending this was normal, pretending this was the same house, with the same rooms as before, in which we might do the things we used to. Like Anton at work, and maybe Anatole at nursery, I moved along and across these surfaces like a ghost. Apart from driving Anatole to nursery and back I rarely needed to leave the house, and until he was home for the night and finding uses for all the different rooms, it was more accurate to say they were not there. What seems closer to the truth is that all the internal architecture was gone, and what stood firm was the part of the house you could see from outside: the warm yellow stonework, the shallow slate roof which over time had accumulated lower and smaller slopes, the outbuilding, the garden shed.

The exterior of the house was not pretending at all. The stone is so old and so settled in its foundations as to almost have grown up from the ground, and it very nearly has. I can imagine the clip, clip, clip of the pick and hammer, the stone splitting and being sorted for size, the weight being laboured onto carts and ambled the few steps down to here, where it stays. Now, we would never move house. It had become our home more than ever before, twinned with its small new annexe in the churchyard nearby.

During these months I inhabited our home as though it were the bare inner shell of that reliable exterior, as though in here were a single cavernous, communal hall, pitched ceiling many multiples higher than the kitchen table, the place I continued to find myself when I had been drifting, as though it were the part of the house closest to the ground, to which the natural pull of gravity saw me descend time and again, being more exposed than usual to the forces of physics.

A cavernous high-ceilinged hall with only a table: I had begun to imagine our home in the image of the mead hall Anton and I had often talked about as we worked on the kitchen. It was a story a thousand years old, of a cold night bitter with icy wind, wild rocking trees, driving rain perhaps. And there in the middle of the cold, one lone room stands against the shattering chill: a mead hall, pagan cathedral to earthly life, warm like honey and raucous with the hum of being alive. Inside, tables of laughter, of drinking honey wine, the resting and easing of limbs from whatever battle there is to fight. And far above, high up in the vaults of the roof, a sparrow chances through an open frame. The beat of its wings draws in the warmth of the fire and the lamps that bristle far below and fill the hall with their glow even this far up. Then another gap lets it out, and it is away again, little feathers rushing against the dark.

It was St Bede who wrote the story of the mead hall. Near the monastery where he worked there were hills like ours, and woods, and perhaps the thought of a hearth-lit hall against the forest night occurred to him there, as I think of it now when

I see our home from the hills at dusk. Watching the clean limit of that warm light, with nothing else around, it is easy to read the meaning he intended: that the span of mortal life and the scale of all we know is nothing more than a little edifice built against the mystery outside. Or even less: just the flight of a sparrow through it.

When Bede was writing, and for centuries before, little birds were trapped by threads sometimes to keep children distracted. There is a long but slender history of painting and drawing showing sparrows detained with a twice-knotted thread, one knot around the finger or wrist of an infant or gripped in its hand, and one around the scrawny ankle of the bird. One painting imagines the baby Jesus transfixed by such a bird, perching astute and serious on the hand of his mother. For this moment each is still, each rapt at the presence of the other.

I knew that rapt stillness. Once, I had been sitting very still in the garden when a sparrow clipped itself to me. There it was, between the knuckle of my thumb and the joint, indifferent. You do not breathe when such a thing happens. You just wait, but wait in a bristling way, every grain of you stretching towards the sensation. Yet I could feel nothing more than the little cold grip

of claws – grave, grown-up, knowing claws, com-
petent claws – and no weight at all. The lightness
of this creature seemed proof that it would not stay
long, as though it hadn't brought its weight because
it wouldn't be here long enough to need it. Then
with a silent scratch it was up, gathering its weight
again to force it against the air and send it darting
into the woods. I realize that ever since then I have
assumed the brevity and skittishness of a sparrow
to be a function of its skeletal architecture. Its
bones are so light as to be composed nearly all of
air; so light that the whole of the skeleton weighs
less than twice its heart. With a frame so slight,
how could it possibly be still?

*

I think of the thread and the sparrow's flight when
I come to Gabriel's grave. I don't know how long
before he will be only his smooth white bones, but
I hope it is soon. I think of the words of the priest
too: words of comfort offered as I stood at the soft
ground of the open grave. He had seldom heard
such a clear declaration of faith, he said, as he
had in the words of the eulogy I gave for my son.
Standing by the coffin and the jar of tulips Anatole

had carried to the altar I had read a few paragraphs, written half in the weeks since Gabriel had died and half before, when he was still alive and I still afraid. I suppose the faith he heard was in these lines, words of comfort of my own, insisting that although we were very sad—

—in an important way, nothing has gone wrong here. Some mysterious quality of Gabriel's cells, there from the very beginning of his life, has brought us all the way to this sad moment. This was the way he was, it was the only way he could have been, and together today we are all honouring him for being just the way he was. He lived as long and he lived as well as he possibly could have, and now, although it's difficult to remember this, he is just where he should be.

At the grave I said thank you to the priest, and unlike the thanks I had granted the undertaker for the toys she put in the cot, this time I really meant it. It wasn't a faith like his I was declaring, but he was right, it was a kind of faith.

Almost every day since Anton had gone back to work I had accepted the pull of gravity towards the kitchen table, and there I had begun to write the story of Gabriel, or rather to write to Gabriel the story of his life and my love for him, my imaginary friend returned to me at last. My imaginary child,

I thought, neither real before his birth nor after his death, and only briefly real between.

But time had passed, and as I continued to write I had begun to understand that I was mistaken. He was not imaginary, nor had he ever been, and nor was he quite the same child as the one I had written to before his birth. He was the same and he was different – not unlike his big brother, it occurs to me, who is always the same child and never the same. I am used to watching how Anatole is new every day, and to greeting his newness every morning when he crawls into our bed. As my body nestles around his growing form I watch him for clues so I can nestle our conversation around his growing mind: clues in the announcements he makes, the elliptical summaries of dreams, each turn of his mind another probing and stretching of the elastic limits of his world. I love these mornings. What must have begun like those constructions of secret thought Gabriel's birth had washed away had, in Anatole's lively mind, been built up by the very tides of life that had shattered his brother's work. Sights and sensations, patterns of language, rhythms of our family life, the sparkling debris of every day seem to cling like flotsam to his ideas and his sayings and are shored up at night in dreams which, I imagine, clarify their structures and strengthen them, and make them more likely to stay.

And as I watched Anatole becoming ever more complicated a creature, ever more familiar and ever more unknown, so, writing at the kitchen table, I understood that his brother was becoming simpler. Or rather, the simplicity of the baby I had imagined before his birth was resolving itself after his death into the subtler quality of being elemental. Gabriel was, I believed, profoundly of the matter of the world, having emerged from matter and then returned to it almost without a breath – and in between, I chose to believe, secure in his mother's arms, all he encountered of the world that was not matter was love.

In my mind this made him a creature composed completely of love. Not only the feeling of love but the material fact of it: the love that is the blooming of life from bonded cells to vaulting structures built on the furthest shores of the mind, the lowing of cattle on the hills, the grace of undifferentiated world, the dark of night and the sea and the pull of the planets into orbit, the love that concentrates in those mealy places that incubate life, among them most of all the womb and the soil. In this way Gabriel was elemental. In this way he wasn't an imaginary friend, he was love itself, squirming and pushing and kicking to take up its place in the world. So I wrote to him, and spoke and wept into the blanket of him. I no longer sang or swayed but still I laid my hands where he had lived, and to the love that he was, I replied, I love you too, just as I had when I used to feel him kick. I love you too, I love you too: here is my declaration of faith.

ELEVEN

The way is narrow out of the churchyard. You unlatch the gate and walk between old walls that seem foreboding until you understand each one to be a world: a dry world but alive with cobwebs and, in the summer, dusty alpine stubs that reach from miniature caverns etched into the stone. Here the walls are too dark and dry for moss, sheltered from rain and sun by the leaves overhead. It is a slow place. There must be insects here, spiders, mice, and they are never seen. Then more light comes as the walls and tall trees part, then gravel and the tarmac of the road to the school, and a couple of houses looking wide out over the field where the mare and its companion Shetland scuff at the grass. You follow the path, and here are other stone walls with alpines that bloom with colour in the summer, and the colour meets the enquiries of bees tumbling methodically in the air and crawling into their caverns among the pearls of leaves succulent with rainwater stored and warmed in the sun.

Then a turn, and you open out onto the hills at last, where the topsy-turvy banks and precipitous slopes are always a surprise. We who live here call them the hills and hollows. We know where the rabbits stretch out in the last of the sun as afternoon turns to dusk, and how quietly to approach from the crest of a certain hill to see them startle and flash away into the cool of the earth. We know which months the cows are brought to pasture, and the dark smell of them and the threat of their weight and hooves and growing horns. We know what time they are fed their grain, what time the dogs are walked, the calls of the preying birds swaying in the sky.

Two years have passed. I stop in the shadow of the oak to rest the loosening ligaments of my joints, halfway home from the churchyard where Gabriel lies. It's almost time to collect Anatole from school, and for the first time I know how it feels for three children to be tugging at my attention. I am pregnant again. Although she is only a few weeks of life so far, and isn't yet real in my mind, I call her a daughter to keep her far away in my imagination from the baby whose home she is beginning to fill. She's barely even a sparrow yet, skeleton still soft, but whether I believe she will really come home, she has already made Gabriel our middle child. I have not greeted her yet, nor begun to sing to her or sway. I dare not press my hands to my waist to imagine her there because I know that if I feel for his absence now, it will be gone.

Instead I talk to Gabriel about her, or rather, I imagine her to him. I imagine to him that she is born and she is well. I imagine carrying her home from the churchyard, the rocking of my pace and the rhyme I hum settling her in my arms. I imagine we're nearly home. As I climb the hill closest to the house, her arms close in and her head lulls heavy against my chest and I know she is asleep. The ground slopes down again but she can't tell, and as I walk, her sleeping thoughts continue to rise. They float up and up, and it's lovely there, bright and still and easy. It must be summer where she's dreaming. From high in the air above us she can see all the hills, the stone of our tall, narrow home, the church, the muddy banks of the river, the round of the horizon, the distant crashing shores that Gabriel saw. She can see herself a child full of life and playing on the hills, big enough to race across their slopes, her eldest brother grown tall and long-legged now and still his joyful self, still that wide, angular smile. He helps her up when it's steep, strides alongside when she speeds down too fast, the two of them fearless in the afternoon sun.

We're nearly home, through the garden gate and almost at the door – but she is still away, far above us, the low rocking of my pace lending her dream the beat of the sun, the adventure of her legs, the speed and the spit of tall grasses grazing her calves as she runs, runs, runs. And around her, all around her, my arms.

Author's Note

If you are reading this book because you have been bereaved or are anticipating bereavement in pregnancy, I am so sorry. I hope you can find some comfort or company in my story, which is, of course, one of many. If you are looking for more stories, in recent years baby loss support organizations have collected hundreds of families' accounts, which are as various in voice and circumstance as the brief lives they celebrate and grieve. You can find many of these in the 'your stories' pages of the Sands, Miscarriage Association and Antenatal Results and Choices websites, among others, and you can search them by subject or keyword if you are looking for families with shared circumstances. If you are looking for advice in this book I'm afraid you may not find much; our own decisions were so finely tuned to the demands of each moment that they are probably of little use to anyone else.

But I have learned two things. Where there are decisions to be made, see that they make sense within the economy of meanings you call your own, whether those meanings come from poetry, faith or science, your community, your family, or the knowledge you hold deep within your body. These meanings will carry you. And know that grief is a thing you can craft. Even when events are cruel and beyond control, in the meanings you derive from them, there is sometimes a whisper of hope, or peace, or grace to be found. Perhaps, in time, this will carry you too.

Credits

Extracts from this memoir have been published in the following scholarly contexts and are reprinted here with permission.

Norwood, T. (2021) 'Something Good Enough', winner of the Wakley Essay Prize, *The Lancet* 398 (10318), 2305–2306.

Norwood, T. (2021) 'Metaphor and Neonatal Death: How Stories Can Help When a Baby Dies at Birth', article in: *Life Writing Journal* 18 (1), 113–124; later reprinted as a chapter in *Essays in Life Writing*, ed. K. Cardell, Routledge (2022).

Norwood, T. and Boulton, J. (2021) 'Reconciling the Uniquely Embodied Grief of Perinatal Death: A Narrative Approach', article in: *Religions* 12 (976).

Norwood, T. (2021) 'Anhydramnios: Birth, Death and Drawing Breath', essay in: *Tendon,*

A Medical Humanities Creative Journal, Issue 04: Breath, Johns Hopkins Centre for Medical Humanities and Social Medicine.

Norwood, T. (2020) 'Creating Bonds with a Baby Expected to Die at Birth', blog post for *The Polyphony,* Durham Medical Humanities Institute: https://thepolyphony.org/2020/10/14/ creating-bonds-with-a-baby-expected-to-die-at-birth/.

Acknowledgements

To my husband and children, thank you for trusting me to tell our story in my words, for your courage as our story unfolded around us, and for your patience afterwards, getting on without me while I wrote very slowly. To our wider family and closest friends, thank you for your company and counsel as we found our way. In the writing of our story, I am indebted to the University of Oxford Centre for Life-Writing, without which this book might have remained a stack of notebooks. Heartfelt thanks to the good old original OCLW writing group, whose friendship and critique sustained the writing from beginning to end, and to John Boulton, Kate Kennedy and Rebecca Gowers, whose encouragement at crucial stages spurred the work on. I am ever grateful to my agent Anna Webber for believing in my manuscript and taking it into her care, and to Susie Nicklin at Indigo for her vision and sensitivity in turning the manuscript into a book. Finally, I owe a debt of gratitude to the many people who helped us through the events of this story. There are too many to name, but I send thanks especially to two midwives at Northampton General Hospital: Maddie, who tended to Gabriel all the minutes of his life, and Louise, who came back at the very end with a blanket all the colours of the rainbow.